501

DATE DUE

MAR 12 2002			
MAY 10 2004			
MAY 28 2004			
OCT 20 2006			
JUN 03 2008			
OCT 20 2010			

MEXICAN AMERICANS

MEXICAN

AMERICANS

JOAN W. MOORE
University of California, Riverside

with
ALFREDO CUÉLLAR

PRENTICE-HALL, INC., ENGLEWOOD CLIFFS, NEW JERSEY

MEXICAN AMERICANS

JOAN W. MOORE

P: 13–579482–X   C: 13–579490–0

Library of Congress Catalog Card No.: 77–113844

Current printing (last digit):

10 9 8 7 6 5 4 3 2

Printed in the United States of America

PRENTICE-HALL INTERNATIONAL, INC., *London*
PRENTICE-HALL OF AUSTRALIA PTY. LTD., *Sydney*
PRENTICE-HALL OF CANADA LTD., *Toronto*
PRENTICE-HALL OF INDIA PRIVATE LIMITED, *New Delhi*
PRENTICE-HALL OF JAPAN, INC., *Tokyo*

Contents

LIST OF TABLES AND FIGURES

Preface

This is a small book about the Mexican American experience in the United States. Only the most important items of background information and the barest outline of recent research findings can be included. Although Mexican Americans are the nation's second largest minority, they are only now beginning to be known outside the region of their traditional concentration—the Border States of the American Southwest. Much more background (and hence more condensation) is necessary than in the case of more "familiar" American ethnic groups.

It is particularly important in this book to include an extra measure of historical background on Mexican Americans and on their region—the American Southwest. Almost no portion of American history is so incompletely covered in the average high school or college course. Though there may appear to be too much material here for a book of this kind, there is actually too little in terms of its importance in understanding the wide range of variations in modern Mexican American communities.

All available demographic information is at least summarized, as is the history of the Catholic church and its Mexican parishioners, Mexican immigration, and Mexican American education.

It is the authors' hope that the interpretations presented in this volume will serve to stimulate a yet more intensive interest among both Mexican American scholars and Anglo scholars. It is our conviction that increased understanding of the population (and of any minority population) can best be attained in the course of mutual interaction—and mutual research. Both members of the minority itself and those outside the minority must participate.

Three groups of Mexican Americans and Anglos interacted to create the perspectives presented in this book. First was a group of colleagues and students, Mexican American and Anglo. Some of these persons worked at one time or another with the Mexican American Study Project at the University of California at Los Angeles or were associated with the senior author at the University of California, Riverside. Next were groups of Mexican Americans throughout the Southwest who

generously showed the senior author their own communities. Their contributions were the mature insights that come only after a lifetime of
attempting to cope with the problems of Mexican Americans in the
Southwest. Third, there were approximately 2,000 Mexican Americans
who responded to surveys conducted by U.C.L.A. in Los Angeles and San
Antonio, and by Operation SER in Albuquerque. These colleagues, students, informants, and respondents (in the process of interaction) helped
create this story of the Mexican American experience. A few persons
helped most particularly. They were Ralph Guzman, Lorenzo Campbell,
Ron López, Thomas Carter, Patrick McNamara, Paul Fisher, and Frank
Mittelbach. Particular gratitude is due Leo Grebler for his extraordinary
qualities as director of the U.C.L.A. Mexican American Study Project
and also for his willingness to comment on portions of this volume and
to make available important data from the project. We also owe acknowledgment to Nicandro Juárez for the assistance and data furnished
by Operation SER, a federal manpower project funded by the U.S.
Department of Labor and the Office of Economic Opportunity.

MEXICAN AMERICANS

The first business in understanding any American ethnic or minority group must always be a hard look at the prevailing popular ideas about that group. These ideas are important: they are clues to the social realities for a group that must live, comfortably or not, inside a larger society. Thus the traits of a group perceived by outsiders are often an artifact of its place inside the larger society and of its meaning for the larger society —and the word for this kind of popular idea is "stereotype."

Classically, a stereotype was defined by Lindesmith and Strauss as a set of assumptions permitting the classification of individuals into groups. They are a set of "beliefs" that "support, justify, and determine the character of interracial relationships." [1]

As we will show in detail in this book, it is probable that the Mexican Americans of today are more diverse in social composition than any immigrant minority group in American history. Thus no minority less deserves simple generalizations, whether they come from the popular press or from scholars. But Mexican Americans have been so judged— quickly and haphazardly—as have all other identifiable ethnic groups in the United States.

Mexican Americans in American Life

Racial myths about Mexicans appeared as soon as Mexicans began to meet Anglo American settlers in the early nineteenth century. The differences in attitudes, temperament, and behavior were supposed to be genetic. It is hard now to imagine the normal Mexican mixture of Spanish and Indians as constituting a distinct "race," but the Anglo Americans of the Southwest defined it as such.[2]

[1] Alfred R. Lindesmith and Anselm L. Strauss, *Social Psychology* (New York: The Dryden Press, 1950), p. 396.
[2] Genetic diversity specifically rules out race as a factor to be considered in the analysis of distinctive Mexican American patterns of health and health care, for example. See A. Taher Moustafa and Gertrud Weiss, *Health Status and Practices of Mexican Americans*, Advance Report 11 (University of California, Los Angeles: Mexican American Study Project, 1968). Definition of the group in racial terms persists, despite denial and suppression. Increasingly, because of the emphasis on black identity, Mexican Americans appear to be consciously confronting their own feelings about being partially Indian. The paradox comes to the surface when a hazel-eyed, pale-skinned man talks about his "Indianness" and a dark-skinned, Indian-featured man talks about his "whiteness." Both "whiteness" and "Indianness" have acquired many dimensions of meaning for

After the absorption of these new Southwestern territories into the United States in the nineteenth century, these alleged racial qualities were used to explain the social status quo, the division of labor in which the Mexicans were frequently on the bottom.

Today very few educated Americans argue that there are any *innate* differences in abilities or character between races. Even fewer accept racial explanations for Mexican American patterns of conduct. However, cultural stereotypes are now quite acceptable, and cultural stereotypes can also serve to justify the status quo: "The Irish are always drunken; it is part of their culture"; "The Italian cultural tradition allows organized crime on the Mafia pattern." Thus the majority gives itself a rationale for differential treatment of Italians and Irish, in spite of the fact that our knowledge of cultural factors affecting the behavior of any ethnic group is not comprehensive, never quite up to date, and never applicable to all new and changing situations. Even basic information on cultural patterns is difficult to assemble. Individual members of an ethnic group are actually unreliable informants about the total subculture, simply because their knowledge is very limited or difficult to articulate. No single family from any cultural group is likely to be representative, particularly in a complex, highly differentiated society like modern America.

It is important, then, to discover what Americans have thought of Mexicans and of Mexican Americans in terms of both racial and cultural stereotypes. How have these conceptions, in turn, been adapted to the actual roles of Mexicans in the society and economy of the American Southwest?

To answer such questions we will draw on the long literary tradition that has emerged from the encounter between Mexican and Anglo. These include reminiscences, official government reports, novels, essays, and academic histories. We also have some present-day interview survey data on how Mexican Americans are seen by others, and how they see themselves.

MEXICANS AS ANGLOS SEE THEM

The first encounters between Mexicans and Americans occurred when the Southwest was still Mexican soil. These first encounters were very important because they fixed the first image of Mexicans that Americans had. Americans came to Texas as colonists with Stephen Austin. They came to what is now New Mexico as traders on the Santa Fe trail;

Mexican Americans, on the basis of interaction within the group and between Anglos and Mexicans diplomatically, legally, and in normal social contacts. (See Chapter Eight for the recent political ramifications of this "race" issue in the Chicano movement.)

to California with the clipper ships from New England; to wilderness areas as explorers; and as soldiers and irregular fighters. In 1836, after a short period of colonization, the Texas American settlers overthrew by violence the Mexican government in Texas.

Whatever their role, Anglos did not hesitate to record their scorn for what they felt to be a backward people in a backward land. They attributed the backwardness to *innate* Mexican traits, one of which was thought to be laziness. "To the early writers the Mexican was just plain lazy and deserved to lose out, as he surely would, to the energetic, productive Northerner." [3] During the Mexican war of 1846–1848 simple hatred crept in. Americans began to call the Mexicans "yellow-belly greasers" and to develop the idea that Mexicans by race were naturally cowards. The belief in the cowardice of Mexicans is commemorated most strikingly in the simplified popular Anglo mythology about the defense of the Alamo. There, during the Texas revolution, overwhelming numbers of cowardly Mexican troops were defied by a small, brave band of Texas rebels. The enormous significance of this event, both in Texas history and in modern relations between Texas Anglos and Mexican Americans, is not in the least affected by the fact that inside the Alamo there were Mexicans fighting with the Americans. The Alamo is a Texas shrine and a standing monument to the Texas belief that Mexicans at heart are a very cowardly people. A second alleged trait is that Mexicans are by nature corrupt. This impression was strengthened by the bloodless conquest of New Mexico; the Anglo legend of the conquest of New Mexico involved Mexican corruption and Mexican cowardice. The Anglo settlers felt simply that a people too cowardly to fight would willingly sell the state of New Mexico. From the guerrilla warfare of this period and later years comes yet a third related image; that the Mexican is unbelievably cruel when he has the upper hand in battle.

But a very different set of images was also appearing during these early years of contact. Such early explorers as John C. Fremont and Major Zebulon Pike met extraordinarily gracious receptions from the Mexicans and reported their contacts with great enthusiasm. Those Mexicans living in what is now California (the *californios*) particularly, were portrayed as living an idealistically pleasurable existence full of warmth, charm, grace, and gaiety. A "great capacity for life enjoyment" was seen to characterize Mexican culture.

Thus certain elements in the Mexican stereotype—positive as well

[3] Cecil Robinson, *With the Ears of Strangers: The Mexican in American Literature* (Tucson: The University of Arizona Press, 1963), p. 33. This book is an exhaustive analysis of the portrayal of Mexican Americans in literature from the earliest contact between Mexicans and Americans through the present.

as negative—were established very early. These images were forged on the frontier rather than in the crowded cities of the East and Midwest; they were established in contacts first on Mexican soil and then in the violent context of the Texas rebellion and the Mexican war of 1848. Because the first contact was made on Mexican soil, Americans were exposed to a full range of social classes, from aristocrat to peon. They encountered cultural styles that ranged from the aristocratic to the primitive. Further, American settlers met Mexicans not only in organized battle but also just as they met the many tribes of southwestern Indians as clever opponents in an almost endless and violent guerrilla warfare.

Although the exposure to upper-class as well as lower-class life meant that the image of "the Mexican" could acquire some social depth, it also meant that the Anglo absorbed the strong Mexican upper-class ideas of race. The upper classes believed themselves to be of "pure blood," pure Spanish untainted by any mixture of Indian blood. Anglos very early began to assume that the aristocratic people and the elaborate fiestas of *rancho* life were "Spanish," whereas the lower-classes were "Mexican." Thus the American conquest was imposed on a society that was the result of a former Spanish conquest and of racial mixture—and racial stereotypes. Anglo acceptance of the already existing prejudices of Spanish America had very important consequences for Mexican Americans.

In later decades the benevolent stereotypes became elaborated. A highly romantic popular literature appeared, which reiterated early themes about aristocratic California life. It is best exemplified by Helen Hunt Jackson's *Ramona*, published in 1884, which depicted *rancho* owners as cultivated, gentle, and exploited. Throughout the twentieth century, American writers continued the benevolent stereotypes whether they wrote about the Mexican Americans of Texas as did Tom Lea and J. Frank Dobie or the poor wage earners of Monterey, California as did John Steinbeck. The strongly folkloric themes of these latter writers appealed to thousands of readers; explicit in these works of fact and fiction is a very real admiration for the Mexican of Cannery Row (Monterey) or the Kineños of the King Ranch (in Texas). The appeal is romantic; it follows a theme, still strong in American literature about the American Indian, of an unspoiled, close to nature, strong, unchanging peasant who follows the simple life without neurotic complications.[4] In the end however, he must fall prey to a more sophisticated and exploiting society.

[4] See Leslie Fiedler, *Waiting for the End* (New York: Stein and Day, 1964). Fiedler discusses the ambivalence in American literature about portrayals of Indians and Negroes. Alternately they represent a lost Eden of strength and innocence and a hell of uncontrolled cruelty and lustfulness. He suggests that such ambivalence permits Americans to project their own unwanted impulses on the members of minorities, and suggests a psychological function of racial stereotypes.

Without overstressing the point, we can see that these racial or cultural stereotypes have certain important social functions, just as in ordinary husband-and-wife relations it may be useful for both parties to play stereotyped roles. Thus a harassed and anxious man may find it enormously comforting to come home to a woman who plays the role of a weak, simple-minded, excessively "feminine" housewife. With such a wife, the husband can maintain an image of himself as "strong" in a highly competitive world.

In general, the enormous demands for achievement in American society may have facilitated the creation of certain stereotypes about subordinate minority groups. To follow this idea out for a moment: the American cultural ideals of achievement are both demanding and guilt-provoking. Americans are supposed to work hard, build, be constructive. The other side of the coin is that they must do so despite human costs. "You can't make an omelet without breaking eggs," the proverb runs. If the eggs must be broken, Americans must cope with the psychic consequences. One way of coping has been to project ego-alien impulses onto visible subpopulations such as the Mexicans. (Ego-alien impulses are so unacceptable to the ego-ideal that their very existence cannot be acknowledged by the individual.) Thus Mexicans became mythically lazy, warm, and possibly savage. In addition, the myth serves to justify their low status in the American West.

On the conscious cultural level, a related logic demands that Mexicans be defined as indolent and accepting. The new Anglo American settlers established ranches and towns and brought in a network of essential administrative and professional services to a wilderness. But another group of people, the Mexicans, did not participate in this work and they did not share in its rewards. For the Anglo Americans the moral equation had to be completed—Mexicans are poor *because* they are unwilling to suffer hard work and boredom. Moreover (so the argument runs), they are quite content with their status; they even prefer the life of the casual laborer and don't really mind poverty. Thus the comfortable Anglo Protestant moral equation of vice and punishment, hard work and material reward can remain intact. Poverty becomes a just return for laziness rather than a reminder of social injustices.

The American Southwest has changed quickly, and Mexicans have been caught up in the changes. But a new generation of writers persists in interpreting what has happened in the light of past stereotypes. John Steinbeck himself provides a hint of this kind of interpretation; when he returns to Monterey in 1960, he is saddened to discover that the "field of love" has become a used car lot.[5] Steinbeck finds his noble Mexican

[5] John Steinbeck, *Travels with Charley* (New York: Bantam Books, Inc., 1962), pp. 198–203.

peasants swallowed by an encroaching urban environment that destroys both land and people. Exposure to the vices of materialistic America will spoil those happy people, the Mexican Americans. Modern romanticism owes much to such visions. The most important legacy of this romanticism is the use of the concept "Mexican culture." We will discuss Mexican culture in some detail in Chapter Seven, noting only for the moment that the liberal who glorifies this selective view of the Mexican heritage shares much (from a functional point of view) with the unromantic conservative who argued that the Mexican Americans were "unassimilable" and lobbied doggedly against Mexican immigration during the 1930s.

The present equivocality of the concept "Mexican culture" is one American symptom of the endless struggle inside all societies that are undergoing rapid change. Values change in all societies. Cultural priorities shift. The search for new meanings and new institutional forms for these meanings has been characteristic of American society (and particularly of American young people) in the decade of the 1960s. Such a search inevitably draws on the resources available in the society, including its highest ideals and variant ideals from the subcultures. A quite new and important notion in American society is that the oppressed are ennobled by injury and thus morally *superior* to the majority. This, along with the notion that the poor can be "spoiled" by materialism, is a significant part of the "new romanticism." It represents a significant continuity with the old romantic legacy; at the present time it means a great interest in the "soul" cultures, Mexican included. There are virtues in this interest; it allows general social norms to be reexamined and possibly some past wrongs to be righted. It also presents some dangers. Witness this warning from a noted psychologist: "Even a remorseful majority . . . must be watchful lest it persist unconsciously in habitual patterns." [6] When "cultural differences" are also associated with poverty and discrimination, members of the dominant system who claim to "respect" and "appreciate" these cultural differences must do so very self-consciously lest they slip into a new kind of paternalism, a psychological exploitation that helps perpetuate the poverty and separation.

MEXICAN AMERICANS AS
THEY SEE THEMSELVES

What do Mexicans themselves think of all this? There has, in fact, been a long history of exploration of Mexican American identity on

[6] Erik Erikson, *Identity: Youth and Crisis* (New York: W. W. Norton & Company, Inc., 1968), p. 305.

the part of Mexican American intellectuals. This exploration has been echoed on the popular level.[7] As we shall show later (Chapter Eight), issues about identity are a major focus of some new types of political activity among Mexican Americans. Until recently, however, there has been little confrontation with the cultural and racial stereotypes held and promulgated by Anglos, despite much intragroup irritation and attempts to redefine these images. Now, rather belatedly, Mexican Americans are reacting, just as did other American subcultural groups before them. Even "José Jimenez" (Bill Dana), the last of the important American dialect comedians, has come under fire. And in 1968, Vicente Ximenes, chairman of the Federal Inter-Agency Committee on Mexican-American Affairs, scolded the television industry for its portrayal of Mexicans as "lazy, shiftless, gun-toting, guitar-playing and barefooted sombreroed men and women" in television commercials.[8] Indeed, the Mexicans have endured as a subject for dialect humor for decades after the comic Irishman, Jew, Italian, German, and Negro faded from the scene. Some of the latter characters disappeared because they just became irrelevant; others, because the comedians were chased away by ethnic pressure groups long after the offensiveness became obvious. (In a related action, as recently as the mid-1960s some Italian Americans formed themselves into a group similar to the Anti-Defamation League of B'nai Brith to protest the portrayal of persons of Italian ancestry as gangsters on television.)

It is reasonable to ask why the Mexicans have been so slow in protesting. Surely one element has been their unfamiliarity with the techniques of protest against bureaucratized mass media. Nor have Mexican Americans ever been employed to any extent in the nation's mass media. Possibly the general tendency to portray Mexicans as "cute" rather than villainous has also kept Mexicans from anger. ("José Jimenez" is depicted as sharp in a peasanty sort of way. The Ford Motor Company used José, complete with a parody of a Mexican accent, to sell Ford Thunderbirds to Mexicans in Los Angeles as recently as 1967.) But then, the image of Stepin Fetchit and Amos 'n Andy were generally "cute" rather than villainous, and it is unimaginable that this form of entertainment would be allowed to persist by the modern Negro community.

We should also know to just what extent Mexican Americans think of themselves and their fellows as a distinctive group as "a people." Identifying persons as "Mexican Americans" *is* important to the larger society. What about Mexicans themselves? First we may note that Mexican Amer-

7 Both traditions are summarized in Ralph C. Guzman, "The Function of Ideology in the Process of Political Socialization" (Unpublished ms.).

8 *Los Angeles Times,* September 20, 1968, p. 21.

icans who are asked what they want to be called by Anglos usually do not want to be called just "American." Most people interviewed in recent surveys in Los Angeles, San Antonio, and Albuquerque wanted to be called "Mexican American," "Spanish American," "Latin American." In short, they see themselves as a distinctive people, rather than as a people or stock fully merged with an all-encompassing American identity. The name they prefer varies from city to city. In 1965–1966, Mexican Americans in San Antonio most wanted to be called "Latin Americans." In Los Angeles most wanted to be called "Mexican" or "Mexican American." In Albuquerque most wanted to be called "Spanish American." In later chapters we will see that each variant has a special historical root and special historical meanings. Contemporary youth movements take the term *Chicano* (a contraction of *Mexicano*) as their term of self-reference. (Formerly this word was almost entirely an in-group term and implied lack of sophistication. This very quality, formerly depreciated, is now exalted as "soul.") Self-designation is perhaps the most rapidly changing aspect of ethnic ideology. In this book we will settle on "Mexican American" and "Mexican" as useful and comparatively neutral terms. This is not in any way to depreciate the attachments to the other names.

But to what extent do Mexican Americans see themselves as Anglos see them—as lazy, volatile, exhibiting a special warmth and love of life, and so on? Our evidence shows that Mexican Americans do tend to agree with features of the Anglo stereotype. More than 80 percent of those Mexican Americans interviewed in Los Angeles and San Antonio felt that Mexicans *are* more emotional than other Americans. More than two-thirds of those interviewed felt that Mexican Americans are less progressive than Anglos—and also that Mexican Americans tend to blame Anglos for what are really their own problems. More than two-thirds felt that Mexican Americans have stronger family attachments than do other Americans. And more than half felt that Mexican Americans are less materialistic than Anglos, but that they also work harder.[9]

   ˙ However, despite the fact that Mexican Americans accept many self-depreciatory stereotypes, they do tend to blame discrimination for at least some of their problems. The extent to which they do blame discrimination appears to vary with the actual level of discrimination in the community. In San Antonio, for example, only a tiny minority of less than 5 percent denied there was discrimination from the Anglo com-

---

[9] Survey data for Los Angeles and San Antonio are from the Mexican American Study Project, University of California, at Los Angeles, household surveys conducted in 1965–66. See Leo Grebler, Joan W. Moore, and Ralph Guzman, *The Mexican American People* (New York: Free Press, 1970), for description of samples and data. Data from Albuquerque are from samples drawn by Operation SER, 1506 3rd Street, Santa Monica, California.

munity. A greater percentage (20 percent) of the Mexican Americans in Los Angeles felt that charges of discrimination (at least in the business world) are unfounded. Thus San Antonio, which probably does have more actual discrimination, is also seen by its minority residents to be more discriminatory than Los Angeles, which almost certainly has less actual discrimination. (A large majority of Mexican respondents in both cities felt that discrimination had decreased in the preceding five years. Only a tiny minority felt that it was getting worse.) ˙

MEXICAN AMERICANS AS A PROBLEM

There is yet another important way in which Mexican Americans fit into American life. In recent years they have been defined more and more as a "problem population." The basic evidence for such a definition will appear in later chapters. We need only note here that disproportionate numbers of Mexicans live well below national standards in education, housing, income, and health. Policy-making agencies have been aware of this for some time. There are increasing numbers of conferences on local, regional, and federal levels, all geared to developing practical solutions for this "problem population." As perhaps one climax of such activity, a series of Cabinet-level hearings were held in El Paso in 1967. Typically, at meetings such as these, spokesmen from the Mexican American community prepare position papers on education, welfare, relations with the police, and other areas of interaction.

Increasingly there are signs that Mexican Americans are also defining themselves as a problem population. In the past, at least among the middle class, there was some reluctance to accept this definition because the idea suggested classification with other "disadvantaged" groups in American society, especially Negroes. Accepting this definition has sharpened the conflict inside the community over self-definition. "Are we a racial or a cultural group?" The latter is the easier definition to accept: thus Mexican Americans are increasingly willing to accept cultural characterizations of themselves and to explain Mexican problems in cultural terms, though increasingly Mexican Americans call for *self*-definition of those terms.

The prime difficulty with explaining a "problem population" in cultural terms is the tendency to overlook certain kinds of data. A cultural image of the "strong Mexican family" leads to complete disregard for the bleak statistics on desertion and divorce. It is still, somehow, a "strong Mexican family" even if it is headed by a deserted and poverty-stricken woman. To other Americans this stress on cultural factors may create the image of a *unique* group, but unique history and culture do not mean unique economic or institutional problems. The cultural explanation may be offered to "explain" a glaring failure in such American institutions as the public school system in terms of the uniqueness of Mexicans, even when it is more reasonable (and possibly more useful for policy intervention) to think in terms of certain situational problems shared with other disadvantaged and low-achieving students. Another example: the near-absence of Mexican Americans in certain professions is sometimes explained by reference to cultural preferences carried to this country from Mexico rather than by any absence of opportunity. Mexican *presence* in certain professions is also explained in cultural terms. (Thus Texas Anglos suggest that the Mexican-American concentration in pharmacy at the University of Texas is a consequence of subcultural values: for example, the supposed importance of folk medicine, the prestige of doctors, and so on. These interpretations are undermined by the fact that pharmacy is far less common as a professional choice in California than in Texas. A more reasonable explanation for its popularity is that pharmacy is attractive as a small entrepeneurship in areas like Texas where there are few other opportunities.)

To put it crudely: both the absence of money and the presence of racial prejudice are easily overlooked in the name of cultural pluralism. "Cultural pluralism," for a group that does not share fully in the rewards of a society, is uncomfortably close to "separate but unequal." On the other hand it would not be useful to produce an analysis of Mexican Americans that was confined solely to a description of their economic situation. It is the objective of this book to present as balanced a view as possible—of culture, situation, and the special subculture that has developed out of their history. Of necessity this view must include all available information on the Mexican cultural heritage, Mexican problems, and the nature of change—both inside the Mexican community and outside in the larger American society.

The history of the Mexican American minority is unlike that of any other American minority group. The only close parallel is with the American Indians, and even there we can find only a few similarities. Mexican Americans *became* a minority not by immigrating or being brought to this country as a subordinate people, but by being conquered. The early history of the Mexican Americans, beginning in the nineteenth century, is thus the history of how they became subordinate people. As we shall see, the process was somewhat different in each of the Border States— Texas, New Mexico, Arizona, and California. This early history, with its very important variations from state to state, set the stage for the large-scale immigration from Mexico in the twentieth century; and it influenced the economic, social, and political roles Mexican Americans were able to play.

It is almost impossible to write a coherent history of any American minority. History is normally written from documents, in which Mexicans become visible only occasionally and then casually only in reaction against some interest or action of the larger society. Except in New Mexico, the Mexican minority has been unrecorded in the economic and social events of American history; the Border States themselves have been remote and isolated from the main currents of American history until very recently. It might even be argued that the sudden appearance of Mexican Americans in the national consciousness today is only one aspect of the sudden appearance of the entire region in a more tightly interdependent national scene.

History: A Minority Appears

EARLY HISTORY OF THE MEXICANS: TO 1900

The history of this minority begins when the Border States passed into the control of the United States. This happened through rebellion (in Texas), after warfare between Mexico and the United States (Texas and New Mexico), and by purchase (Arizona and New Mexico). Between the Battle of San Jacinto in 1836 and the Gadsden Purchase of 1853, the United States acquired the present states of Texas and New Mexico and parts of Colorado, Arizona, Utah, Nevada, and California.

In all that vast stage at that time there were no more than a handful of actors. If we look at the approximate number of Mexicans in each state when it was first taken over, we can begin to understand something of the very diverse experience of Mexicans in each area. There were perhaps 5,000 Mexicans in Texas, 60,000 in New Mexico, no more than 1,000 in Arizona and perhaps 7,500 along the length of California.[1] There were also some settlements in what is now modern Colorado, but they were too small and isolated to be considered here.

Generally the Mexican colonists had settled in a pattern resembling the ribs of a giant fan; they had entered the Southwest through mountain passes and river valleys. The "fan" their settlements formed stretched more than 2,000 miles along its northern edge, but in only a very few places did it extend more than 150 miles north of the Mexican border. These first Spanish settlers established small, tight, defensible clusters in strategic valleys, fertile river areas, and other typical frontier locations. Three factors nearly always dominated the choice of site: the availability of water, transportation resources, and protection from marauding Indians.

From the first years protection from Indians was essential. There might well have been as many as 120,000 Indians ranging through these territories. For most of the nineteenth century the Indians, particularly the successful Apache tribes, held much of this area by force, thereby helping to isolate and to keep intact the existing Mexican-Spanish institutions and settlements. Carey McWilliams writes, "From 1848 to 1887, the Anglo Americans were so preoccupied with the Indians that they had little time left to devote to the settlement of the region or the exploitation of its resources."[2] More important, the interminable ambushes, battles, and massacres made the Mexicans welcome the protection of the American troops, particularly in the territories of New Mexico and Arizona. But by 1886 the last of the Apache raiding parties either came under U.S. control or went across the border into Mexico. Then the Anglo American settlement of the Southwest could begin.

Texas

The frontier of original Mexican settlement in Texas ran no further north than the Nueces River, north and east of which the hostile Comanches prevented further advance. There was considerable Mexican settlement even in the dangerous area between the Rio Grande and the Nueces rivers, but most Mexicans (probably 80 percent) lived in the lower Rio

[1] See Carey McWilliams, *North from Mexico* (Philadelphia: J. B. Lippincott Co., 1949), p. 52; and U.S. Bureau of the Census, *Historical Statistics of the United States, Colonial Times to 1957* (Washington, D.C.: Government Printing Office, 1960). McWilliams' book remains the best general history available.

[2] McWilliams, *North from Mexico*, p. 53.

Grande valley and in the river cities, with El Paso the most westerly town of any consequence. Such present-day south Texas counties as Starr, Zapata, Cameron, and Hidalgo thus had thousands of early residents. In west and south Texas the population grew rapidly from about 8,500 in 1850 to 50,000 in 1880 and 100,000 in 1910, in spite of the fear and dislocation caused by the many wars, large and small. (During one episode of the Cortina War in 1859, for example, a slice of lower Texas 150 miles long and from 50 to 75 miles wide was invaded and devastated by Mexican horsemen.) Texas was also the only part of the border area that was seriously involved in the Civil War.[3]

The economy of this area depended upon the large cattle ranch but in an early form common in the Border States, which was based upon the ownership of livestock rather than land. After the annexation of Texas, the Anglos easily assumed their role of landowners (between 1840 and 1859 all Mexican-owned grants but one in Nueces county passed into the hands of Anglo settlers).[4] Mexican *peones* were available for labor on these ranches. Meanwhile, along the Rio Grande a series of mercantile towns grew up (Brownsville, Dolores, Laredo, Rio Grande City, Roma) to handle the commercial needs of this area. Although all of these river towns had some Anglo residents and some Europeans, most were almost entirely Mexican. Here early appeared some Mexican middle-class elements, which were to be important in the future as the valley of the Rio Grande became more Anglicized. The change came very slowly; as late as 1903 Brownsville held only 7,000 persons, mostly Mexican. At that time Corpus Christi was not yet a deep water port and numbered only 4,500 persons.[5] To a large degree the Mexicans of the Rio Grande valley and the river towns were still dominant numerically.

However, the large cattle and sheep ranches of south and east Texas were very soon fenced, following the invention of barbed wire in 1875. Enclosure was of major importance because cutting a fairly unrestricted cattle range into small pieces tended to freeze out a large number of small and medium-sized cattle and sheep ranchers, including both Mexicans and Anglos who owned livestock but little or no land. A few years

3 Juan Cortina is still a hero to many Texas Mexicans. He had the aura of the folk-avenger. Eventually Cortina achieved great political power in northern Mexico. During the Civil War invasion of Texas by U.S. troops he "assisted" Union troops in attempting to stop the smuggling of cotton and contraband war material. This assistance added nothing to harmonious relations between Texas and Mexicans. For a description of Cortina, his career, and the state of semi-war in south Texas, 1855–1875, see Tom Lea, *The King Ranch*, Vol. 1 (Boston: Little, Brown And Company, 1957).

4 Paul S. Taylor, *An American-Mexican Frontier* (Chapel Hill, N.C.: University of North Carolina Press, 1934), p. 294.

5 Arthur J. Rubel, *Across the Tracks. Mexican-Americans in a Texas City* (Austin: University of Texas Press, 1966), pp. 34–35.

later cotton plantations slowly moved into south Texas from east Texas, continuing a movement toward the west and cheap new land that was long characteristic of cotton culture. However, cotton required a great deal of hand labor and this time there were no Negro slaves to follow the new plantings westward. The resulting demand for cheap Mexican labor to cultivate cotton, either as wage laborers or as tenants, was so great that it fixed, very nearly in its modern form, the economic fate of the Mexican immigrant and the Mexican old settler in Texas. A few Mexicans would succeed in achieving ownership of the land they worked, but not many.

By 1890 the cotton culture of the deep South was well established in Nueces county. The attractive prices for good cotton land, the high profits in "brushing out" and cultivating former pastureland, and the availability of cheap labor from across the border doomed all but a few of the old cattle ranches in south Texas in a very few years. By 1900 the Mexican laborer in both rural and urban Texas had become defined as an inferior person and as a member of a distinctive race entitled to neither political, educational, nor social equality. Remnants of Mexican equality survived only to a limited extent in some of the commercial towns of the Rio Grande valley where Mexicans remained in the majority.

New Mexico

The Texas pattern of economic subordination of Mexicans extended west into the grain and ranching area of eastern New Mexico, an area that is still called "Little Texas." As large cattlemen began to enclose their land and to push out Mexican and Anglo sheep ranchers, enough friction was generated to produce the famous Lincoln County wars from 1869 to 1881.[6] Some Mexicans did retain their holdings, although serious overgrazing in nearly all areas of New Mexico had damaged this form of economic enterprise well before 1900.

New Mexico entered the period of Anglo settlement with its share of Mexican colonization centered in three types of inhabited areas: military and administrative towns (such as Santa Fe and Albuquerque), large ranches, and a considerable number of small villages. Most of the villages depended heavily on agriculture and livestock ranching. Isolation and continual warfare with the Indians meant that Anglo inroads came very slowly; in 1848 there were about 60,000 persons in the territory and virtually all of them were Mexican. Most, in fact, lived either within a 50-mile radius of Santa Fe or on the headwaters of the Rio Grande and

---

[6] Nancie L. González, *The Spanish Americans of New Mexico: A Distinctive Heritage*, Advance Report 9 (University of California, Los Angeles: Mexican-American Study Project, 1967).

Pecos rivers.[7] Unlike those in the borderlands of Texas, New Mexico's Spanish-speaking residents had a full range of class structure and a well-established ruling group, able in every respect and interested in retaining political power. The territorial legislature was thus dominated by "Spanish Americans" (actually members of no more than 20 prominent families) from its establishment until statehood in 1912. For 64 years an alliance between the wealthy Spanish and certain Anglo interests in banking, ranching, and railroading effectively controlled New Mexican political life through the infamous "Santa Fe Ring." [8]

New Mexicans lived for the most part a considerable distance from the border and were not greatly disturbed by the endemic border warfare and raids that characterized south Texas. Not until the coming of the railroads was movement throughout the territory easy in any direction, and not until 1886 was it easy to pass back and forth across the border because very large stretches of this area were held by Apache raiders.

Nonetheless, economic changes were swiftly breaking down this small and curiously isolated Mexican society. By 1900 overgrazing and erosion, the consolidation of larger ranches, a steady division of lands among heirs, and the rapid withdrawal of grazing land to various types of federal use (railroads, homesteading, and national forests) forced many, perhaps most, small herders and farmers into wage labor. At the same time some degree of immigration coming west from Texas swelled the labor pool and tended to reduce wage rates. Thus, long before the turn of the century, the New Mexican villager was fighting a slow but losing battle against pauperization. The full effect would not be felt for several generations, but the decline of sheepherding was obvious; this primary and traditional activity of New Mexicans was disappearing and with it a form of social organization many years old.

New Mexico was slow to develop discrimination against and isolation of the Mexican minority. As Nancie Gonzalez writes, "Inter-marriage between Anglo men and Mexican women was apparently quite common, and not restricted to any particular social class. Business and commercial mergers between Anglos and Mexicans occurred frequently, and in politics, coalitions of Anglos and Mexicans worked together in each of the major parties." [9] But there is evidence that this tolerant mood began to change by 1900 as, inevitably, more and more American settlers and important American mining, ranching, and transportation interests flowed into New Mexico. Railroad lines had opened the territory quite effec-

[7] González, *Spanish Americans of New Mexico*, p. 29.

[8] The Santa Fe Ring was an alliance of Mexican and Anglo interests that dominated the economic and political life of New Mexico for a period after the Civil War.

[9] González, *Spanish Americans of New Mexico*, p. 57.

tively by 1881. The new railroads allowed dozens of isolated company towns to exploit the considerable mineral resources of New Mexico with Mexican labor. The new markets for wool, meat, and hides opened by the railroads accelerated the consolidation of larger and more efficient ranches. Continuous enclosure slowly destroyed the smaller sheepherders and the smaller cattlemen. Thus the very forces that spelled economic opportunity to large Anglo enterprises were forcing a considerable portion of Mexicans into the status of a dependent minority.

Arizona

In Arizona settlement began north from the Mexican state of Sonora in the seventeenth and eighteenth centuries with a chain of missions that opened the valleys of the San Miguel, Altar, Santa Cruz, and San Pedro rivers. Some colonization followed, mostly in the form of large estates. But these estates were subject to continuous raids from Indians. Thus, when in 1751 troops from Mexico were withdrawn for a time, Apache raiders laid waste to the entire province, an area covering nearly all of modern Arizona. A military stalemate was just barely restored in succeeding years and then slowly the Indians gained the upper hand again until by 1856 nearly all Arizona colonists lived (for safety) in the fortified city of Tucson.

In Arizona the shift to Anglo domination was less painful than elsewhere because there were so few resident Mexicans. By the 1880's the final collapse of Indian resistance coincided very closely with the beginning of large-scale mining and the building of the railroads. The few Mexicans in Arizona were not nearly numerous enough to supply the endless appetite for cheap wage labor. Thousands more were imported through the labor markets of the border towns of Laredo and El Paso. Thus the Texas pattern of transition to wage labor appeared very early in Arizona—and with it the dreary succession of lynchings, unsolved murders, and vigilante actions against a working-class population of what was defined as a different race.

Arizona settlement patterns are notable for the large number of isolated mining towns, nearly all of them with a large majority of Mexicans. Some Mexicans were natives; some were imported. Some probably followed the mines as they were opened and closed by a single company in different areas. These company towns appear in large numbers in the 1880s, nearly always extremely isolated places as Tubac, Miami, San Manuel, Mammoth, Walker, Dewey, Morenci, Duquesne, Metcalf, Ajo, Bluebell, and scores of others. Some are still in existence; others are ghost towns. Miners' enclaves also provided the original impetus for many larger Arizona towns, such as Bisbee, Prescott, and Douglas. Typically the mining towns were totally isolated from the normal American society of the time. Many were too small or too dominated by a single employer to provide any but the most rudimentary public services. From the beginning there was rigid separation by occupation, which meant segregation of the Mexicans from the Anglos, with such additional forms of segregation as "Mexican" shopping hours in the company store.

Copper was Arizona's single most important mineral product, and its exploitation expanded rapidly with the nation's needs for electrical equipment. There was also some cattle ranching in Arizona, and some cotton farming, but ranching and agriculture were hazardous and very expensive enterprises in a country so arid. Generally both were conducted on a grand scale by large companies. A territory so dominated by a few economic interests was also dominated politically by the same interests. It could not have been otherwise in a remote western territory. Territorial governments have been summarized as "poor government by a remote Congress which was not responsible to the inhabitants; limited appropriations mainly for military posts, the Indian service, roadbuilding, and mail routes; and inadequate and frequently corrupt administration." [10]

California

California was the most westerly province in the great fan of original Mexican settlement—so far west, in fact, that its principal economic partner was not Mexico but New England, via the clipper ships of the nineteenth century. Here during the Mexican hegemony a handful of *rancheros* held an enormous area, separated almost completely from Mexican centers of control.[11] Mexico generally ignored its westernmost province and even failed (beyond an occasional shipment of felons) to settle it in any substantial numbers. Most of the resident Mexican population approved of the idea of annexation by the United States. Mexico was weak; there were endless petty quarrels with Mexican officials; there were serious troubles with Indians in southern California but no help from Mexico and the ranchers were long accustomed to trade with the United States. Thus the "Bear Flag" rebellion of 1846 was welcomed, as was the succeeding military occupation by U.S. troops.

The early occupation was amiable enough, but meanwhile gold was discovered in the interior, and suddenly northern California was being "settled" at tremendous speed by Anglo miners; at least 100,000 miners were arriving each year. Massive immigrations of Sonorans from Mexico

10 From an unpublished manuscript prepared by Paul Fisher for the Mexican-American Study Project (Los Angeles: University of California, October, 1967).

11 This account is based substantially on Leonard Pitt, *The Decline of the Californios: A Social History of the Spanish-Speaking Californians, 1846–1890* (Berkeley and Los Angeles: University of California Press, 1966).

and Chileans (13,000 Latin-Americans in 1849 alone) complicated the problem. The Anglo miner of midwestern or southern origin felt that "a greaser is a greaser" even if he owned 35,000 acres of land and was pure Castilian. In the mines, remote from any law, Mexicans were taxed, lynched, robbed, and expelled in an endless series of incidents. Many of the Mexicans and Chileans then drifted into California towns and formed a substantial group of landless laborers. The mining troubles were an early and a bad precedent for American-Mexican relations in California.

Very soon the gold mines became less profitable and the new arrivals turned to agriculture, squatting on the Mexican grants in large numbers and filling California courts with endless and complicated title litigation.[12] Many of the Mexican grants had been of dubious legality from the beginning, and others were often "floated" (or extended) in court to cover all nearby improvements and available sources of water. There was considerable violence in some northern counties between squatters and owners. At one time 1,000 armed squatters near Healdsburg ambushed surveyors, the Mexican owners, and a sheriff's posse with complete impartiality. Within a few years the *californios* (Mexicans living in what is now California) had lost nearly all economic power in northern California. Not all the land claims were decided against them, but the steady and growing influence of Anglo settlers left them in the position of a small, tightly knit group of overextended landlords, barely able to hold their lands, and hated by most of the community. Although California became a state in 1850 and the government was more decentralized, more powerful, and more responsive than in either Arizona or New Mexico, the land troubles in northern California were beyond the capacity of government on any level to resolve.

In southern California the situation was completely different. There were very few important changes for nearly a generation after the Gold Rush. Mexican *rancheros* owned the land; the Indians did the work; the Anglo settlers were few and unimportant. Most of arable southern California was owned by no more than 50 men and their immediate families, including a group of about a dozen Mexicanized Yankees. The availability of both Indian labor and cheap land worked against the development of a Mexican lower class, either on ranches or in towns. Nor was there yet a large number of immigrants; no economic enterprise in southern California needed any appreciable quantity of wage labor, although

---

[12] State reports in 1849 showed that 200 California families owned 14 million acres of California in parcels ranging from 4,500 acres to about 50,000 acres. Against this concentration, the American white settler invoked the Jacksonian idea that a few men of immoderate wealth and special privilege wasted the land and denied industry its due. Pitt, *Decline of the Californios,* p. 87.

a few Mexicans worked in the "dry" gold mines of southern California. (The railroads before 1875 used Chinese and Indians for laborers.) Southern California also was spared the Anglo squatter because northern California offered a more humid climate and family-sized farms. The squatters found arid southern California unattractive.

Although the ranchers shared power in local and state government and their economic base held firm after 1850, this generation watched uneasily as racial tension grew noticeably. Los Angeles was inhabited by an explosive combination of lower-class Mexicans, Anglos, Indians, and Chinese, and it soon became almost impossible to maintain even a façade of racial harmony in an era of strong anti-Catholicism, nativism, and frequent violent crime. Even the state became less tolerant: taxes were imposed upon land; laws were no longer published in Spanish; in 1855 a law was passed forbidding school instruction in Spanish.

The *rancheros* responded by pressing hard for the separation of southern California from northern California (along a line near San Luis Obispo) but this effort was doomed when the local issue became entangled with national questions of sectionalism and slavery. The final blow, however, was economic. In 1862 a devastating flood was followed by two years of extreme drought. This disaster very nearly destroyed California's Mexican wealth at its source. Mortgages, legal fees, taxes, and low cattle prices completed the ruin. According to Leonard Pitt, before the catastrophe of the 1860s practically all land parcels worth more than $10,000 were held by old families, mostly Mexican. By 1870 these same families held barely one-quarter of these large parcels.[13] Politically the erosion was reflected by the gradual disappearance of *californios* from public life; by the early 1880s there were no longer any Spanish names in the public offices of southern California.

The final blow (as in all the Border States) was the arrival of the railroad, which reached as far west as San Francisco in 1869. In 1876 the railroad was completed to Los Angeles from northern California; the next year, a line to Los Angeles from the East was finished. In 1887 alone the two new railroads brought in more than 120,000 Anglo-American settlers. There were by that year only 12,000 Mexicans in all of southern California. Thus, almost in one year, the Mexican majority became a local minority. A fierce land boom after the arrival of the railroads ended most of what remained of Mexican ownership of the great ranches and transferred the land to the not-too-gentle management of financiers, railroad developers, town planners, cooperative colonizers, and irrigation companies.

13 Pitt, *Decline of the Californios*, p. 248.

This was roughly the state of the Mexican Americans in the border states by 1900. In general, their first massive contact with Anglo settlement (normally settlers brought in large numbers by the new railroads) coincided with their subordination, even if it did not immediately cause it. Everywhere except in New Mexico, this charter-member minority (a minority status acquired by conquest rather than immigration) was by 1900 hopelessly inundated by the tide of Anglo immigration, reduced to landless labor, and made politically and economically impotent. Socially the long-settled charter-members had become "Mexicans" indistinguishable from the new immigrants from Mexico. Perhaps more important, by now all Mexicans, whatever their isolation from other Mexican communities, had in common a heritage of racial conflict. Only in New Mexico did the Mexicans retain numerical plurality and some degree of control in political affairs.

LATER HISTORY OF THE MEXICANS:
AFTER 1900 TO
THE GREAT DEPRESSION

By 1900 the basic Mexican settlements were well established. In nearly every city where there would be a sizable urban Mexican population, its rudiments had appeared by the turn of the century. After 1900 the history of Mexican Americans is inextricably bound with the movement of the Border States into the mainstream of the American society and the American economy.

Agricultural Technology

The first great force changing the Southwest was that of agricultural technology. The age of cattle in these states came and went rather quickly, destroyed by overexpansion both of herds and of land holdings, by competition from more efficient ranchers, and by droughts and severe winters. After the arrival of the railroads, ranching was followed by a boom in dry-farming (farming without irrigation), which ended disastrously in a series of great droughts throughout the West after 1885. An immediate result of these droughts was the realization in Congress that the key to large-scale settlement of the Border States would be water. Thus the Reclamation Act of 1902 authorized a series of expensive reservoirs designed to provide irrigation water for certain areas. Irrigated farming is intensive farming—highly capitalized, with heavy labor requirements, year-round production, and crop specialization. No poor farmer or homesteader could possibly own or maintain such land. An acre of lettuce required more than 125 man-hours of labor per crop and an acre of strawberries more than

500 man-hours.[14] Melons, grapes, citrus fruit, sugar beets, cotton, vegetables: all required the initial investment for irrigated land and then the costs of brush grubbing, deep plowing, leveling, extensive planting and, in the case of citrus, a long wait for a first crop.

As a result, the demand for cheap Mexican labor grew at a rapid pace. With the arrival of factory farms came further work: crating, packing, processing, and shipping. These new irrigated farms—and the work on them—were to dominate the conditions of life of the Mexican minority in the Border States as decisively as the working patterns of coal mining once dominated wage labor in Appalachia.

Cotton continued to move steadily westward from Texas and then, suddenly, with the coming of irrigation it spread into the Mesilla valley of New Mexico (1910–1920); into the Gila and Salt river valleys of Arizona (1908–1909); into the Imperial valley of southern California (1910); and into the San Joaquin valley of central California (1920). Mexicans followed in every case as migratory workers or as seasonal workers who lived nearby. It was a pattern repeated in hundreds of towns in five large states, including a good portion of eastern Colorado. But the migratory labor story is too well known to repeat in detail here; it was—and is—a pattern of low earnings, miserable health and housing conditions, child labor, and virtually no contact with the Anglo world beyond the labor agent (or smuggler) and the grower, together with a squalid "Mextown" somewhere near the fields.

The railroads also needed cheap labor—so much, in fact, that most of the Mexican laborers who entered the United States in the first two decades of the century may have worked on them. Because much railroad work is seasonal and many workers left to remain in towns newly opened by the railroads, recruitment of labor was continual. In sum, "since 1880 Mexicans have made up 70 percent of the section crews and 90 percent of the extra gangs on the principal western lines which regularly employ [in 1930] between 35,000 and 50,000 workmen in these categories. In 1930 the Santa Fe reported that it was then employing 14,000 Mexicans; the Rock Island, 3,000; the Great Northern 1,500; and the Southern Pacific, 10,000." [15] Typically, Mexicans were assembled in El Paso and then sent out on six month work contracts. (In 1908 some 16,000 Mexicans were recruited in this one Texas city.) Section hands and extra crews lived on the rails or in boxcars. Where these boxcars settled for a while, a small colony of Mexicans appeared. There were soon hundreds of these remote shantytowns scattered throughout the Border States, West, and Midwest.

[14] Lawrence Leslie Waters, "Transient Mexican Agricultural Labor," *Southwest Social and Political Science Quarterly* 22 (June, 1941), pp. 49–66.

[15] McWilliams, *North from Mexico*, p. 168.

For the Border States this steady flow of labor was vital, and legislative and political pressure made sure it kept arriving. Sugar beet recruiters from other states (notably Colorado) so angered Texans that the Texas Emigrant Agent Law of 1929 made this type of recruiting illegal. (It was still done illegally at the rate of about 60,000 Mexicans a year.) The theft of workers was common, as was the practice of selling the same work crew more than once. "Crews of imported Mexicans [in 1915] were marched through the streets of San Antonio under armed guard in broad daylight and, in Gonzales County, workers who attempted to break their contracts were chained to posts and guarded by men with shotguns," reports McWilliams.[16] Many, if not most, of these workers were smuggled across the border. Thus Texas served as the main reservoir of cheap wage labor for sugar beet harvesting in the North, the central states, and the West; interurban electric railway construction and fruit picking in California, cotton harvesting in Arizona, and wage labor in the tanneries, meat packing plants, and steel mills of Chicago. Mexicans appeared in the automobile factories in Detroit, the steel mills of Ohio and Pennsylvania, the mines and smelters of Arizona and Colorado, and in railroad maintenance everywhere.

In Texas and elsewhere an important by-product of this traffic in labor soon appeared. It became customary to employ "reliable" Mexicans to hire and transport this vast flow. Slowly, an upper working class began to appear, based on the need for straw-bosses, foremen, and labor recruiters. In the fields themselves the workers sometimes moved into more skilled work: operating vehicles or equipment, handling processing machinery and even clerical tasks. The older communities in the Border States also supplied an array of small ethnic services: all the restaurants, rooming houses, small retail stores, and personal services required by a flow of workers.

Public Land

The second great force, particularly apparent in New Mexico, was the pattern of public land usage. Timbercutting, overgrazing, and incautious dry-farming by a flood of Anglo homesteaders threatened the land itself. Accordingly, the allocation of land for national forests began in New Mexico as early as 1892, and many small villages found themselves cut off from grazing lands used for generations. Ultimately an eighth of the land in New Mexico passed into restricted usage. Other large grants were made to railroad companies, amounting to 20 million acres in California alone. Still other tracts were restricted to aid education, forming land

---

16 McWilliams, *North from Mexico,* p. 179.

grant colleges. In Arizona the same process stifled even the beginnings of self-sufficiency for small stock operators and small farmers.

Conflict

The third important force shaping Mexican American life after 1900 was the almost unending racial and international conflict in the Border States of both the United States and Mexico. The northern Mexican provinces traditionally spawned revolutions, and inevitably some of the conflict spilled over the border, particularly into the New Mexico and Texas borderlands. By 1911 there was internal turmoil in Mexico. Without going into the details of the strange German effort to involve Mexico in her 1917–1918 war against the United States (by reviving an old Mexican dream of "recovering her lost provinces") it can be said that between 1908 and 1925 the Texas border was in nearly continuous conflict. Mexico itself had had relative peace only during the 35-year regime of Porfirio Diaz. After downfall of that regime in 1911 a full-scale revolution developed, with fighting so continuous, so chaotic, and so violent that the "Mexican government" (when it existed) could neither control border raids into the United States nor protect the lives and property of its own citizens from American reprisals.

El Paso provides one example of the strategic importance of the border for relations between the two countries at this time. It was a center for arms shipment to all partisans in the Mexican revolution, just as it shipped refugees and contract laborers to all corners of the Border States. A full-scale American "Punitive Expedition," commanded by General John J. Pershing, entered Mexico in 1916. *Villista* raids (raids by followers of the Northern Mexican revolutionary, General Pancho Villa) on Columbus, N.M., Nogales, Ariz., and four towns in Texas (Dryden, Eagle Pass, Glen Springs, and Boquillas), prompted the invasion.

On the domestic scene, the years before and just after World War I brought a great deal of labor conflict involving Mexicans in the United States. Some of these strikes and protests were extremely violent, although neither frequent nor coordinated enough to destroy the Anglos' belief in "Mexican docility." Of course it is not difficult to imagine that during the period of international conflict between the United States and Mexico, Mexican laborers in the Border States should have acted with circumspection. Nonetheless, in Ventura in 1903 more than a thousand Mexican and Japanese sugar beet workers went on strike. In 1913, a particularly ugly strike-connected riot at Wheatland, California attracted national attention. Soon after, in 1915, three unions of Mexican miners, numbering about 5,000 men, went on strike at the Clifton, Morenci, and Metcalf mines in Arizona. Also in 1915, Arizona miners struck the mines at Ray.

At Bisbee there was a violent strike in 1917. In 1920 Mexican workers struck the Los Angeles urban railway. In later years the strikes in the fields and mines of the Border States were both more numerous and more sophisticated. The earlier ones were significant, however, because Mexicans were generally denied normal channels of political expression in any of the Border States except New Mexico. The alien, of course, had no voice, but the settled and native-born were also efficiently disenfranchised, either by means of the poll tax and the open primary (as in Texas) or by simply being overwhelmed in numbers and by political manipulation (as in California).[17]

Mexicans soon became a topic of controversy within the legislatures of the Border States and in Congress as well. The Mexican labor pool continued to grow. More federal irrigation projects, particularly in Arizona, and the rapid extension of fruit farming, cotton, and intensive year-round truck crops into California kept the supply of labor always slightly less than the demand. The massive and irresponsible manipulation of this politically voiceless minority depended on the domination of state legislatures by the big agricultural, railroad, and mining interests.

However, World War I had begun to change things for the Mexican laborer and to remove him from complete economic dependence on these three industries. Urbanization was speeded up, and the wartime industries provided high wages for a few years to some Mexican Americans who learned skilled trades. The resultant loss of workers in agriculture was filled temporarily by more Mexican immigrants, but this immigration could not last forever. By the early 1920s some important signs of strain appeared: Congress was considering restrictionist legislation.

It was in the testimony on the quota legislation considered in 1924 and 1925 that the political implications of the changing situation in the Border States became evident and the political power of the big economic interests was challenged. The growers had always believed that—since their workers vanished from *their* sight at the end of the work season—Mexicans went "home to Mexico." ("The Mexican is a 'homer.' Like the

---

[17] The idea may seem strange to the modern "progressive" or liberal, but the political reformers of the Populist and Progressive age were strongly anti-minority and anti-alien. Thus their ideas for political reform had very little direct effect on Mexicans in the United States. The Populists in Texas made no effort whatever to reach the Mexicans in Texas, and in 1913 the California Progressives worked in the state legislature to pass a child labor law, old age pensions, and oddly, an alien land bill to deprive 331 Japanese farm owners of their land. The latent Progressive hostility to Mexicans became evident when Senator Albert Beveridge led a bloc of Progressives in Congress in opposing Arizona and New Mexico statehood, because they felt the large Mexican population of these territories was unfit for full citizenship. (In evidence of this obviously prejudiced argument was the undeniable fact that Mexican votes were manipulated in both territories as well as in Texas.)

pigeon he goes back to roost," a farm lobbyist told Congress.[18]) But the cities had evidence that this was not so: city taxpayers throughout the Border States were becoming aware of how much these "homing pigeons" were costing to support when they were unable to find agriculture work. In 1925, Riverside, California spent 90 percent of its welfare budget on Mexican cases, and much larger Los Angeles spent 28 percent of its 1927 charitable funds on Mexicans, who were only 7 percent of the population.[19] The hearings in Congress accurately reflected new realities in the Border States, and the changed political significance of the Mexican minority. Within the decade the strains were to produce massive deportations, detailed in the next chapter.

It took some time for the changing situation to work its way into the conscious imagery relating to Mexican Americans. For generations, Mexicans had been seen as a necessary part of the Border States' extractive industries, yet as primarily alien and locked forever into a relationship to the land that could be either romantic or sordid, depending on the observer's point of view. But by 1920, Mexicans were exhibiting many of the desires shown by other and earlier immigrant groups: they wanted economic security; they liked (or were forced) to live in urban areas, and whenever possible their children went to school and abandoned agricultural labor. Just as the development of the northern Negro ghettos went largely unnoticed, however, so the urbanized Mexican (whether newcomer to the city or charter member) was at the time largely invisible. Sometimes the swift spread of urban areas enveloped small colonies of Mexicans, whose actual style of life was relatively unaffected by the process. Sometimes the rapid urbanization meant the development of slums near the city's center and a new, though generally ignored, "urban problem." The full measure of these changes can probably never be traced because of the inadequacy of data—particularly of census returns—for the years involved. Nonetheless, all the most important forces affecting the Border States during these years tended to push Mexicans into the cities —and to make the image of the Mexican as a rural farm laborer less valid.

THE EMERGING MEXICAN MINORITY: THE DEPRESSION AND AFTER

The deepening agricultural depression of the 1920s was followed by the Great Depression. The resulting stagnation hurt Mexicans as much as any other minority group dependent upon wage labor. In the cities,

---

[18] Carey McWilliams, *Factories in the Field: The Story of Migratory Farm Labor in California* (Boston, Mass.: Little, Brown And Company, 1939), p. 127.

[19] McWilliams, *Factories in the Field*, p. 148–49.

the burden of Mexican welfare cases became increasingly onerous. Few Border State cities were prepared to handle any substantial amount of social welfare during the early years of the Depression. Many were particularly vulnerable to the economic stresses of the Depression because they lacked a well-diversified economic base. Although the cities had grown rapidly in the years preceding the Depression, they were simply not large enough nor financially strong enough to cope with massive relief loads. Throughout the area, and also in the Midwest, cities began to implement the suggestion that the growers had made during the Congressional debates of the previous decades—that the Mexicans be "repatriated." [20] Thus the Mexicans may have been the group most severely and most directly hit by the economic problems of the Border State cities.

Things were not much better in agriculture. In Texas, cotton became so unprofitable that vast areas of the Texas Panhandle and west Texas turned from cotton to cattle, reversing a historic process. Falling prices hurt the small farmers substantially and the Mexican small farmers among them, accelerating their collapse in the long competition with larger, more efficient mechanized farms. There were further complications. The famous Dust Bowl migrations into the Border States, particularly into California, and the movement of many urban workers, both Anglo and Mexican, to agriculture (sometimes under pressure from urban relief agencies) drastically cut down the amount of agricultural work available to the unskilled ethnic. Half of California's farm labor in 1934 was native white: no more than a third of the field workers were Mexican.[21] Wage rates fell drastically, as did farm prices. Isolated areas that depended upon a single crop or product (south Texas on cotton farming, the San Joaquin valley of California on citrus fruit, southern Arizona on copper mining) were seriously damaged when employment was sharply cut down. The persons most severely affected were the unskilled and the relatively immobile or unadaptable. Many of these were Mexicans. In New Mexico (a state that suffered severely) a group of New Deal surveys revealed just how much the agricultural problems of New Mexico had pushed the Hispano *rancheros* into wage labor. Unfortunately, there was suddenly almost no wage labor available. Nancie González summarizes one of the findings of an important study by the Department of Agriculture in the Tewa Basin of New Mexico:

> In 11 Spanish-American villages containing 1,202 families, an average of 1,110 men went out of the villages to work for some part of each year prior to 1930. In 1934, only 157 men out of 1,202 families had found outside

[20] A valuable unpublished manuscript and documents on the Los Angeles repatriations of the 1930s were supplied by Ronald López.

[21] McWilliams, *Factories in the Field*, p. 305.

work. When this situation occurred, they tried to fall back upon the more traditional sources of income—farming and sheepherding—and then discovered that changes in the ecological balance, new laws, and competition with modern techniques made it impossible to support the existing population.[22]

Federal programs took up some of the slack, most spectacularly in New Mexico, where a *majority* of the Spanish Americans were directly dependent upon the federal government. Foreclosures and tax sales removed still another large portion of the indigenous landowners. In general the response of the New Mexicans to the extreme economic deprivation of the Depression was twofold. They joined the migratory labor army following the crops throughout the Border States, and their families moved into nearby cities to reduce the risk of starvation. The effects of increasing urbanization began to be apparent in these years. We learn in New Mexico, for example, that in the village of San Geronimo, 15 miles southwest of Las Vegas, more than one-third of its 58 houses were deserted before 1940.[23] In yet other areas of the Border States the story of rural depopulation was repeated, if less spectacularly.

Several other factors worked to complete the economic decline of the Spanish Americans in New Mexico. First, many Anglo Texans and others from southern states emigrated into the eastern plains area of the state. Second, there was heavy immigration of Mexican nationals into the mines and fields of New Mexico, and these workers competed for jobs with the older residents. Third, there was a striking volume of Anglo American immigration into New Mexico from other parts of the nation after the 1920s. Inevitably the Anglo newcomers (particularly those from Texas and the other southern states) confused the older charter-member residents with the new immigrants from Mexico. As Nancie González points out, a considerable amount of racial discrimination followed, an attitude quite new in New Mexico. At this time begins an intensified effort by the native inhabitants to distinguish themselves from the new immigrants. Hence the important distinction between "Spanish American" and "Mexican." [24]

It was during the years of the Great Depression that the New Deal and the Democratic party won the undying allegiance of Mexican Americans. More important, however, during the Depression the attitudes of both business and labor toward Mexicans (and minorities in general) reversed completely. Business opinion stopped claiming that the Mexicans were a necessary source of labor. On the other hand, labor interests

22 González, *Spanish Americans,* p. 88.
23 González, *Spanish Americans,* p. 90.
24 González, *Spanish Americans,* Chap. 8.

stopped blaming immigrant Mexicans for the prevailing low wages and made some organizational gains among them. Nevertheless, despite symbolic gains, it seems probable that the New Deal efforts to provide a minimum of economic security for impoverished segments of the population affected Mexican Americans only peripherally, mainly when Mexicans left rural areas for industrial employment in the cities.[25]

The gradual improvement in economic conditions between the end of the Great Depression and the beginning of World War II left the newly urbanized Mexicans in a much better position. The cities offered superior education, even if it was often segregated. Cities offered a greater variety of work opportunities and much greater contact with Anglo society and its varied institutions and agencies. Most important, it was becoming increasingly clear that Mexicans were to be permanently on the scene, and this acknowledgment that Mexicans were here to stay was important, even if they were seen as unacculturated and nearly unassimilable. As Thomas Carter notes, during the 1930s educators in the Border States began to set themselves the task of acculturation rather than simply evading their responsibility for educating Mexican Americans.[26]

In Los Angeles and San Diego this consciousness of a new minority was exacerbated and made urgent as a consequence of the famous "zoot suit" riots and "pachuco" disturbances of the early 1940s. As with the race upheavals of the 1960s among blacks, the disturbances discredited all former assumptions about the minority, nearly destroyed an older generation of Mexican spokesmen by revealing their impotence, and ended forever the convenient myth in such cities as Los Angeles that the real Mexican leaders centered around the Mexican consul. The riots in Los Angeles (publicized nationally as instigated by the Mexican youth gangs) left a residue of deep bitterness and shame in the Mexican community. It was to be years before the full story of the riots, with the racist activities of servicemen and policemen, became widely known and before they came to be generally acknowledged as race riots.[27]

World War II offered Mexican Americans new opportunities. Between 300,000 and 500,000 men served in the armed forces and thus saw both the United States outside their isolated five-state ghetto and also significant parts of the rest of the world—where Mexicans had never been considered an inferior people. Many others learned skilled trades in the defense employment boom and changed residence permanently. In New

---

[25] Fisher, see footnote 10 above.

[26] From an unpublished manuscript prepared by Thomas P. Carter for the Mexican-American Study Project (Los Angeles: University of California, October, 1967).

[27] See McWilliams, *North from Mexico,* for an account of the riots and other problems of Mexican Americans in Los Angeles.

Mexico perhaps a fifth of the rural population of Mexican origin may have left the state.[28] By 1950 the Border States were even more completely urbanized than the rest of the United States. Mexican leaders frequently trace the beginnings of general self-awareness to the social changes brought on by the war. By this time a steady and accelerating migration from Texas to California had begun. Slowly, also, the choice of entering immigrants from Mexico shifted from Texas to California and from rural areas to cities. The exchange of information, the broadening of experience, the increasing ethnic awareness, all meant a shift away from areas of more restricted economic and social opportunity.

Large-scale importation of cheap Mexican labor in the form of *braceros* began once more during World War II. This new wave of agricultural immigration, tailored to the needs of the growers, had less overall impact on the Mexican Americans than had the earlier immigration, largely because in fact most of the *braceros* did "go home" to Mexico when the agricultural season was finished. Furthermore, there was some degree of governmental supervision over their living standards, which had some indirect beneficial effects on Mexican Americans living in some of the more discriminatory towns in Texas. However, when the war ended, both legal and illegal immigration began again on a large and increasing scale. And this time the widespread opposition to cheap labor and the declining power of Border State agricultural interests combined to produce the second great deportation of Mexicans—"Operation Wetback." This time the question was not indigence but illegality. In five years there were 3.8 million deportations of Mexicans (only 63,515 under formal proceedings), although it was common knowledge that many if not most deportees returned to the United States, perhaps to be deported again and yet again.[29]

It is also from the World War II era that most of the signs of Mexican-American political self-consciousness date. A more aggressive political style characterizes the organizations formed at the time; on many local scenes there were protests against some of the more flagrant acts of discrimination practiced in the Border States. Very slowly, the results of decades of isolation had become obvious to the Mexican Americans, and increasing efforts were made to change the situation within the context of the American political and legal systems. (See details in Chapter Eight.)

[28] William W. Winnie, Jr. "The Hispanic Peoples of New Mexico", unpublished Master's Thesis (University of Florida, Gainesville, Fla., 1955), p. 97. Cited in González, *Spanish Americans of New Mexico*, p. 89.

[29] These deportations are also discussed in the next chapter as part of the history of immigration from Mexico. For details, see Leo Grebler, *Mexican Immigration to the United States: The Record and Its Implications*, Advance Report 2 (University of California, Los Angeles: Mexican-American Study Project, 1966).

But as indicated in the first chapter, neither ethnic self-consciousness nor Anglo recognition of Mexican problems is as yet fully developed. From the minority side, there is continued diversity in outlook and self-conception, the product of generations of isolation from other Mexican Americans as well as from the larger society. Isolation bred diversity, and a history of racial conflict and impoverishment increased the isolation. The gradual emergence of Mexican Americans as an American minority is the end result of a century and a half of contact.

Mexican American life was shaped by the land in which they settled. In many ways the geographic, economic, social, and demographic peculiarities of the American Southwest were decisive factors. Mexican American life was also shaped by the manner in which they entered the Southwest: patterns of immigration determined to a very large extent when Mexicans would enter and who would enter. Who, then, were the immigrants? When did they enter the United States? How was immigration controlled? How will patterns of immigration change in the future?

THE BORDER STATES: BACKGROUND FOR A MINORITY

Any group entering the American Southwest [1] in the late nineteenth century would have faced a peculiar situation. Paradigms of assimilation and acculturation derived from American contacts with immigrants in the East and Midwest simply are not relevant. Some of the peculiarities of the Border States tended to result in dispersal and isolation of the Spanish-speaking populations, particularly the immigrants. Other and perhaps weaker

The

Origins

of Diversity

factors tended to push the immigrants from Mexico and the "charter member" Mexicans into a common pattern.

Geography and Economy

Among the peculiarities that tended to scatter enclaves of Mexicans, the vast spaces of the Border States may have been decisive. Even today the two most concentrated areas of Mexican American population in the United States are more than a thousand miles apart, separated not only

---

[1] The phrase "American Southwest" is used as a convenience and because of its identification in the American mind with the old "Spanish Southwest." Terms for this region are various and often confusing. Texas is a major center of Mexican American population and yet is a true part of the deep South. California, Arizona, and New Mexico belong to the West. Again, New Mexico, Arizona, and Colorado are Mountain states. Colorado is not properly a southwestern state, although its early population of Mexican Americans means that it is generally included in any figures covering the entire Southwest. Accordingly the term "Southwest" will be used throughout to refer to the five states of California, Arizona, New Mexico, Texas, and Colorado. The term "Border States" will include California, Arizona, New Mexico, and Texas—all states sharing the Mexican border.

by sheer distance but by massive mountain ranges and desert lands hundreds of miles in width. Only a few highways and railroads connect these areas today. Before 1880 there was no east-west through passage whatever. It was inevitable that the small settlements, beginning in the latter part of the sixteenth century and continuing throughout the seventeenth and eighteenth centuries, would be effectively isolated: from each other, from the centers of population in Mexico, from the weak U.S. territorial governments—and even today, from the federal government in Washington.

The Border States also offer Mexican Americans comparatively easy access to the homeland. We shall discuss control of the border later in this chapter; but despite increasing administrative control it is normal and natural even today that all manner of intercourse should occur easily across the border. By contrast the Negro cannot return "home"; he has no home except in America; European and Asian immigrants are far from home. But most Mexican Americans still live within a short driving distance of Mexico.

Still another peculiar condition affecting the Border States is their economic climate.[2] These states were slow to develop economically—and, in fact, thus retained until very recent years their reliance on agriculture and mining. This economy, heavily oriented toward the exploitation of natural resources, required much capital (which had to be imported from the East) and vast quantities of cheap and unskilled labor. There were few European settlers in these states in the nineteenth century. Accordingly a succession of non-Europeans served as cheap labor, coming either as temporary contract laborers or as immigrants. Thus Mexicans followed large groups of Chinese (until 1882), Japanese (until 1907), Filipino, and even Hindu workers as the chief supply of labor. The housing and control of such workers, in gangs or in groups of families, meant the construction of labor camps and cheap housing near work sites but nearly always remote physically, socially, and politically from the mainstream of Southwestern life. A pattern of workers' enclaves, of pockets of isolation—the direct result of the economy of the Border States—was firmly established and has left many traces.

The Border States were much more slowly urbanized than the rest of the United States. In 1900, 70 percent of the population of the American Southwest was rural, a proportion considerably higher than in the East or the Midwest. By 1940 the proportion of urban and rural residents approached equality, and, surprisingly, since that date the process of

2 This account of the social, political, and economic milieu of the Border States draws heavily upon Leo Grebler, Joan W. Moore, Ralph Guzman, *The Mexican American People* (New York: Free Press, 1970), Chap. 4.

urbanization throughout the Border States has rushed ahead of that in the United States as a whole, although quite unevenly within the area. Thus the Mexican American population was caught up quite late in one of the most significant national trends of this century.

Politics

The Border States were also very slow to reach political maturity. All except Texas and California were territories for many years, and New Mexico and Arizona did not attain statehood until 1912. (The recency of these events is suggested by the fact that Arizona's first senator, Carl Hayden, still served in the U.S. Senate as recently as the mid-1960s.) Throughout the Border States political organization was late and relatively unstructured by what the East and Midwest define as normal political party activities. There was never much opportunity for any ethnic group to duplicate the success of Irish, Italian, and Jewish immigrants in the urban areas of the East in influencing the objectives of local or state government. Moreover, party organization in these states is generally moribund between elections. At no time has there been any counterpart of the urban ward system so characteristic of Eastern cities. Thus there was no training ground for the political game, no recruiting process for ethnic leadership as there had been for some other American ethnic groups. The heritage for Mexicans has been delayed entry into politics, and a parochialism and a sense of ineffectuality in organizational and political activity.

Furthermore, as indicated in the previous chapter, state governments in the Border States were for many years dominated by a relatively few economic interests.[3] The railroads, the powerful mining companies, the owners of the big "factory farms" and the big land development companies controlled Border State governments for many years and are today a powerful influence. In the past, however, such an alliance between business and politics meant that a politically unsophisticated minority group could be easily manipulated. The late formal structuring of state and local government has also had unfortunate effects on Border State law enforcement. All too often the weak and undermanned local authorities became the arm of private interests, for example, in labor disputes. Even today in Texas the well-known Texas Rangers are sometimes used in labor-management disputes involving Mexican Americans, an action quite in keeping with their historical record of violence against Mexican Americans.

[3] This account uses material prepared by Paul Fisher for the Mexican American Study Project (Los Angeles: University of California, November, 1967).

Internal Diversity

The Border States also present a remarkable and often bewildering social and economic diversity. Local social systems differ considerably and the effect of a wide range of opportunity and of toleration for Mexicans has been enormous. In California, a relatively rich and well-developed state, the variation from city to city ranges from the relatively open and industrialized society of San Francisco and Oakland to the social system of the nearby San Joaquin Valley, in whose large cities the Mexican minority is still quite rigidly segregated. Santa Fe is a world apart from the nearby isolated villages in the northern valleys of New Mexico in terms of Mexican American life. Then, as an extreme range from either, the life of the Texas border cities of El Paso, Laredo, and the string of cities from Brownsville to McAllen is conditioned by the presence of a huge population of Mexican Americans. In 1960 the percentage of Mexican Americans in El Paso was 45 percent; in Laredo, 82 percent; in the Brownsville-Harlingen-San Benito metropolitan area, 64 percent. Many smaller towns along the Rio Grande are almost all Mexican.

A few indicators of the range of social acceptance, economic opportunity, and governmental concern will be sufficient—income, political participation, and educational achievement. The median annual income of Mexican American families in the San Francisco-Oakland Standard Metropolitan Statistical Area (SMSA) in 1960 was $6,308. (Though very high for Mexicans, this was still below the Anglo median.) This is an area that is highly developed economically and reasonably open to its minorities. By contrast, the median family income of Mexican Americans for the same year in the Brownsville-Harlingen-San Benito SMSA (a Texas border area) was $2,206.

Political participation is more difficult to appraise, but the most casual inspection shows that Mexicans living in Texas have a very small political voice, especially in local affairs.[4] Many remained completely disfranchised up to 1966, the year the poll tax was abolished. Nonetheless in 1967 two Texas Mexican Americans were elected to Congress. Considering that there are about 1,400,000 Mexican Americans, forming

[4] For example, the Mexican American attempt to wrest control from Anglos in Crystal City attracted national attention in the early 1960s. With some outside assistance, the Mexicans gained control in 1963, by winning all five city council seats. But three councilmen were removed from office soon after for nonpayment of taxes and utility bills; the mayor was harassed by the Texas Rangers, and outside help evaporated: two years later a Mexican-Anglo coalition government was elected—still a substantial change from the previous regime. The uproar attending this "rebellion" indicates how firmly entrenched local power is in such small Texas towns. Several studies have been made of the Crystal City case. See Leo Grebler, et al., *Mexican American People,* Chap. 23.

14.8 percent of the Texas population, this is not a great accomplishment. In New Mexico, by contrast, the Mexicans carry an important tradition of political activity, supplying state legislators and even U.S. Senators with fair regularity. Until World War II the "Spanish" population of New Mexico actually outnumbered the Anglo residents. In New Mexico a large number of small cities and a dispersal of political power to rural areas (typical of other states as well as New Mexico) tended to work in favor of the minority group.

Access to education is yet another important index of the comparative ability of existing agencies of government to meet the needs of a minority population. In general, the Mexican-American minority is shockingly undereducated, but the range in educational attainment is also impressive. The median years of school completed by Spanish-surname persons over twenty-five years of age varies from 8.6 years in California to 4.8 years (less than the fifth grade) in Texas. It is not likely that this wide range in educational achievement reflects any important difference in ambition or ability between the two groups of Mexican-Americans. The difference, rather, is the ability or the desire of the school system to teach Mexican-Americans. (See Chapter Five.)

Population Characteristics

Demographic factors have also worked to create a peculiar climate in the Border States: it is possible they have significantly increased a climate of racial intolerance. First, through most of this century these four states have had an importantly higher proportion of native whites in the Anglo population than in the rest of the United States. This is true, for example, at each census date from 1910 to 1960, although the difference narrows each year until 1960. Texas and New Mexico have the highest percentages of native whites, although the proportion varies in different areas at the moment and has, in fact, always varied in the past from area to area.

The second demographic reality in the Border States is that Mexican Americans are forced to share their minority status with several other groups. In all Border States, except Texas and California, there have always been large numbers of American Indians. In Arizona's first census in 1870, Indians outnumbered whites four to one. There are also very large numbers of Orientals. In California, to illustrate this point, the nonwhite population in 1910 was 5.0 percent, of whom only 0.9 percent were Negroes; 0.7 percent were Indian and 3.4 percent were Orientals. By 1960 the nonwhites had grown to 8.0 percent, of whom most were Negroes (5.6 percent), only a few (0.2 percent) Indian, and a considerable number still Oriental (2.2 percent). In later years the Mexican Americans increasingly found themselves sharing the bottom of the economic ladder with the American Negro. The growth of California's present Negro population began only during World War II, and although the proportion of Negroes in the Texas population has been declining, Texas was still 12.4 percent Negro in 1960. These demographic factors are important, first because the Anglo population of the Border States has faced *several* racial minorities (contact that preconditioned their relations with Mexican Americans), and second because the minorities themselves have frequently and increasingly been placed in competitive relations with each other.

Yet another factor in the Border States populations has been important to Mexican Americans. This predominantly Roman Catholic minority confronted an Anglo population that was substantially more Protestant than in most other parts of the nation. The percentage of Protestant whites in these states can be estimated at about 88 percent, against 12 percent Catholics. Of the non-Catholics, an extraordinary proportion, particularly in Texas, are oriented toward fundamentalist Protestantism. No other American religious group would be so likely to be hostile to the Catholic church, with its hierarchy, ritualism, and priestly control. (As it happened, this stereotype of the Catholic church was not very accurate in the Border States, as we shall detail in Chapter Five.)

This uncongenial combination of population elements produced antagonism very early in the region's history, as we discussed in the previous chapter. No other part of the United States saw such prolonged intergroup violence as did the Border States from 1848 to 1925. Even the relationship between Negroes and white Southerners offers no such overt conflict, which involved Indians and Asians as well as Mexicans. The extent of the violence—cattle raids, border looting expeditions, expulsions, deportations, lynchings, civil riots, labor wars, organized banditry, filibustering expeditions, revolutions—can hardly be exaggerated. Some of these minor and virtually unknown conflicts laid waste to entire counties and lasted for years. Thus the myth of broad, free and easy frontier tolerance so cherished in the Southwest obscures the real fact of continuous and acute racial tension.[5]

These are some of the physical, social, economic, and demographic peculiarities of the Border States. Later in this chapter we will trace the impact of some of these peculiarities upon a growing minority. But there is yet another factor—of prime importance—that so dominates Mexican

[5] No complete or even partially complete listing has been made of these endless frontier and racial conflicts. Neglected bits can be found in any regional history or in scholarly publications dealing with Western history.

life in the United States that it must be considered separately and carefully. Vast numbers of Mexicans poured into the United States after 1900 in the last of the great waves of immigration to enter this country, which further conditioned the story of the Mexican American minority.

IMMIGRATION: A CLOSE
AND OPEN BORDER

From Tijuana-San Ysidro on the coast of California to Brownsville-Matamoros on the Gulf of Mexico runs the long border of more than 2,000 miles that separates Mexico and the United States. Sometimes the border is a real barrier and heavily guarded. Sometimes, as in the Big Bend area of Texas, nature makes it almost impassable. More often it is not much more than a high wire fence and dirt road running through southern San Diego county, through the lower end of California's Imperial valley, and then across vast desert regions in southern Arizona and New Mexico to El Paso. Here the border becomes nothing much more substantial than the Rio Grande, a river that is one of the nation's longest but often shallow enough to wade across and sometimes (in dry seasons) disappearing altogether.

In this century this boundary has deeply influenced the life of Mexican Americans. The closeness and accessibility of the United States meant that a flow of immigrants constantly pressured the economic achievements of Mexicans already in this country. Then, also, the river frequently shifted channels, bringing to the affected area a rash of quarrels about property rights. Water rights in this very dry land were of critical importance and the subject of many quarrels between American and Mexican citizens and American and Mexican cities and provinces. This border is indeed a sharp contrast to that shared by the United States and Canada.

The origin of the border is itself worth some detail. Under the terms of the Treaty of Guadalupe-Hidalgo (February 2, 1848), Mexico ceded a vast territory to the United States. The line of demarcation following the Rio Grande was clear enough, but west of El Paso the treaty negotiators followed a faulty map. The ensuing arguments very nearly caused a second war. Ultimately James Gadsden was sent to Mexico City to negotiate a new acquisition. The original line of treaty would have followed the course of the Gila river across Arizona, a natural and reasonable line, but Gadsden managed to secure by purchase an additional 45,532 square miles. The new border ran south of the Gila and secured for the United States a substantial area for a proposed railroad line to California. Furthermore, as it happened (and no Mexican thinks it accidental) the Gadsden purchase of 1853 included some of the world's richest copper mines.

But the real consequence of the Gadsden purchase was an unnatural border. Long-established commercial ties between the Mexican state of Sonora and Arizona were legally severed. A vast inland area was left without a seaport (Guayamas would have been a natural outlet). Some established cities were split in half, surviving to the present as "twin cities." Further east, where the Rio Grande marks the border, the instability of the river channel generated quarrels among people who had to share the river in order to live.[6] Thus history left the two nations with a difficult border.

History of Immigration

For some reason the massive and ceaseless movements of people over this frontier have attracted very little serious study. There have been only two studies of consequence, one in 1930 and one in 1966.[7] This neglect is hard to understand in light of two facts: first, there were huge numbers of immigrants. (During the one decade 1954–1964 more people entered the United States as immigrants from Mexico than from any other country.) Second, there have been almost continuous political and legislative wrangles about the United States-Mexican border and its control, and such quarrels are unusual in American history.

Mexican immigration differs from the much better known European immigration in many ways. It may be well to abstract some of these distinctive features before proceeding with a history of the immigration. First, it has never been regulated by formal quotas; we will discuss this point in detail shortly. Second, immigration from Mexico, though continuous, has been massive only recently—and is the only recent prolonged massive movement. Third, Mexican movement across the border has followed some very complicated patterns—some very informal. There are permanent legal and permanent illegal immigrants. Many Mexicans, some of them U.S. citizens, live in Mexico and commute to work daily across the border. Agricultural workers enter on contract or for seasonal employment. There are important flows of businessmen and tourists from both countries, and there are border area residents with business interests

[6] As Carey McWilliams states, "From El Paso to Brownsville, the Rio Grande does not separate people: it draws them together." McWilliams, *North from Mexico,* p. 61. Much of this account of the early border is based on McWilliams' work.

[7] Manuel Gamio, *Mexican Immigration to the United States* (Chicago: University of Chicago Press, 1930) and Leo Grebler, *Mexican Immigration to the United States: The Record and Its Implications,* Advance Report 2 (Los Angeles: University of California, Mexican American Study Project, 1966). This account draws heavily on Grebler's material.

on both sides of the border. Through the many years when the border was comparatively open there was always a substantial "backward" movement.

Fourth (and this is related to the third point) it has been comparatively easy for Mexican immigrants to reach the United States. The large and economically attractive cities of the Border States, especially those in Texas, were accessible by railroad, highway, and bus. It is relatively easy for both failures and successes to return home, and has been relatively easy for a prospective immigrant to make a trial journey to the United States.

Fifth, no other minority was ever deported from the United States as massively as the Mexicans. Sixth, no other minority except the Chinese has entered this country in such an atmosphere of illegality. A long, relatively unguarded border and recruiting by important economic interests insured that in some years perhaps three times as many Mexicans entered illegally as were admitted legally. No accurate estimate is possible, but the consequence was inevitable; the illegal aliens and their communities were peculiarly vulnerable to economic and social discrimination of all kinds.

Statistically it is impossible to analyze Mexican immigrants earlier than 1910. We know that an important movement took place after 1848 when thousands of Mexicans joined in the California gold rush. The chaotic condition of the border areas until 1886 prevented any government control whatever over the population movements between the two nations. Arizona, for example, was dominated by the Apache throughout most of the nineteenth century. Formal control over this human traffic began in 1886, but records were so approximate as to be nearly valueless. Not until 1907 was a definite control pattern set up. As late as 1919 the entire border was patrolled by only 151 inspectors, most of whom were actually serving at 20 regular ports of entry. Before 1954, when control was stepped up, Galarza suggests that Border State legislators succeeded in keeping Border Patrol appropriations too low to accomplish more than the most rudimentary control, thus permitting the flow of cheap labor so necessary to the southwestern economy.[8]

By 1907–1908 Mexican railroads linked interior Mexico with the border cities. This made immigration much easier, though there was not an immediate increase in the volume; most immigrants were agricultural laborers, and debt peonage, still a prevailing pattern in Mexico, kept many immobile. It was only after the sudden dissolution of peonage during the revolution after 1910 that a substantial movement to the

[8] Ernesto Galarza, *Merchants of Labor: The Mexican Bracero Story* (San Jose, Calif.: The Rosicrucian Press, 1964), p. 64.

United States began. Then, from 1910 to 1920, the immigrants apparently included a significant number of middle-class and upper-class Mexican refugees, many of whom hoped to return to Mexico.

In addition, from 1910 to 1919 American labor requirements in the Border States were increasing. The Chinese had been excluded in 1882, the Japanese in 1907, and the supply of European immigrants to the United States suddenly waned with the beginning of World War I. World War I greatly spurred both prices and demand for agricultural and mine products, both specialties of the Border States. Special regulations were issued in 1917 to admit "temporary" farm workers, railroad maintenance workers, and miners. The word "temporary" had the usual meaning: in June, 1919 one report showed that two-thirds of an initial group of 30,000 Mexican workers admitted after 1917 simply remained in the United States.

This first wave of immigration in 1910–1920 was only a beginning; the next decade saw Mexican immigrants arrive in massive numbers. In 1920 there were 51,042 legal immigrants—a number large enough to raise fears in Mexico that the big neighbor in the North was pulling away far too many people. In the United States there was also some apprehension, leading to stricter administrative controls in 1929. The figures themselves tell the story, as given in Table 3–1.

In the United States there was an expanding demand for agricultural labor, while at the same time in Mexico the disruption attending the revolutionary wars prompted much of this immigration.

The influx slowed markedly after 1929. American agriculture was suffering from a prolonged decline even before the more general economic drop of the Great Depression. Further, the Mexican economy was beginning to recover from the revolutionary period. In the United States other sources of cheap farm labor became available as the migration from the Dust Bowl to the West began and as a growing number of urban workers sought refuge in farm work. By 1930, Mexican immigration dropped to only 11,915 legal entries.

The drop is only partially understandable as a response to impersonal supply-demand factors. More importantly, it reflects the impact of massive efforts to send the Mexicans "home," where, it had always been assumed, they "belonged."

U.S. Immigration Service officers stepped up the search and deportation procedures for illegal aliens. Various devices including the stoppage of welfare payments, were employed to encourage legal residents to undergo "voluntary" repatriation. Most disturbing, in many cities of the West and Midwest, Mexicans who applied for relief were referred to variously named "Mexican bureaus." The sole purpose of these agencies was to

TABLE 3–1

NUMBER OF MEXICAN IMMIGRANTS TO THE UNITED STATES
AND ALL OTHER IMMIGRANTS, 1910–1967

Fiscal Years	Mexican [a]	All Other	Fiscal Years	Mexican [a]	All Other
1910	17,760	1,023,810	1939	2,265	80,733
1911	18,784	859,803	1940	1,914	68,842
1912	22,001	816,171	1941	2,068	49,708
1913	10,954	1,186,938	1942	2,182	26,599
1914	13,089	1,205,391	1943	3,985	19,740
1915	10,993	315,707	1944	6,399	22,152
1916	17,198	281,628	1945	6,455	31,664
1917	16,438	278,965	1946	6,805	101,916
1918	17,602	93,016	1947	7,775	139,517
1919	28,844	112,228	1948	8,730	161,840
1920	51,042	378,959	1949	7,977	180,340
1921	29,603	775,625	1950	6,841	242,346
1922	18,246	291,310	1951	6,372	199,345
1923	62,709	460,210	1952	9,600	255,920
1924	87,648	619,248	1953	18,454	151,980
1925	32,378	261,935	1954	37,456	170,721
1926	42,638	261,850	1955	50,772	187,018
1927	66,766	268,409	1956	65,047	256,578
1928	57,765	249,490	1957	49,154	277,713
1929	38,980	240,698	1958	26,712	226,553
1930	11,915	229,785	1959	23,061	237,625
1931	2,627	94,512	1960	32,684	232,714
1932	1,674	33,902	1961	41,632	229,712
1933	1,514	21,554	1962	55,291	232,472
1934	1,470	28,000	1963	55,253	251,007
1935	1,232	33,724	1964	32,967	259,281
1936	1,308	35,021	1965	37,969	296,697
1937	1,918	48,326	1966	45,163	323,040
1938	2,014	65,881	1967	42,371	361,972

Source: Leo Grebler, *Mexican Immigration to the United States: The Record and its Implications,* Advance Report 2 (University of California, Los Angeles: Mexican-American Study Project, 1966), p. 106. Based on Annual Reports of the U.S. Immigration and Naturalization Service and its predecessor agencies, which are the source for supplementary figures for 1965–1967.

a By country of birth.

get Mexicans off the relief rolls by deporting them. The possibility that a Mexican might be an American citizen was never considered. This move was organized by local authorities with small regard for the niceties of immigration law, or, for that matter, constitutional rights. Mexican authorities cooperated, and the Mexican American (citizen or new immigrant) who wanted to stay in the United States had no recourse. Carey McWilliams witnessed one of these "repatriations" in Los Angeles:

> It was discovered that, in wholesale lots, they could be shipped to Mexico City for $14.70 per capita. The sum represented less than the cost of a week's board and lodging. And so, about February 1931, the first trainload was dispatched, and shipments at the rate of about one a month have continued ever since. [1933]. A shipment consisting of three special trains left Los Angeles on December 8. The loading commenced at about six o'clock in the morning and continued for hours. More than twenty-five such special trains had left the Southern Pacific Station before last April.

> The repatriation programme is regarded locally as a piece of consummate statecraft. The average per family cost of executing it is $71.14, including food and transportation. It cost Los Angeles county $77,249.29 to re-patriate one shipment of 6,024. It would have cost $424,933.70 to provide this number with such charitable assistance as they would have been *en-titled* to had they remained—a saving of $347,468.41.[9] [Emphasis added.]

Again, complete figures are not available,[10] but in the four years between 1930 and 1934 more than 64,000 Mexican aliens left the United States without formal proceedings. Altogether the repatriation and sharply reduced immigration cut down the Mexican-born population in the United States from 639,000 in 1930 to a few more than 377,000 in 1940.

Only a few years later, however, the manpower emergencies of the early World War II years made the Mexicans welcome again. Immigration rose slightly but steadily, and workers were once again actively recruited, this time through the famous *bracero* (contract labor) program of 1942. For a time after the war, importations under this program stopped; but agricultural employers were able to build such a strong case for resuming the *bracero* program that in 1951 Congress enacted Public Law 78, which replaced the earlier executive agreements. The employers' arguments were familiar: the urgencies of the Korean War made them persuasive. In sum, it was argued that there were not enough domestic workers and that native Americans were unqualified or less effective for the stoop labor needed in the fields or both. Labor unions and public welfare organizations offered counterarguments without much effect.

If the *bracero* program was meant to slow down the steady flood

[9] Carey McWilliams, "Getting Rid of the Mexicans," *The American Mercury*, March, 1933.

[10] Immigration records on departing aliens are so confused as to be nearly useless. Departures are reported as cases, not persons. They may include non-immigrant aliens. After World War II departures were listed only as "passengers departed," a category that simply includes international passenger traffic of all kinds. Grebler, *Mexican Immigration*, pp. 27–28.

of "wetbacks," it was a resounding failure. Again no data is available about illegal entries except some speculation that the ratio of illegals to legals might run as high as four to one. Expulsions from the U.S. continued at a rate that shortly reached 100,000 persons a year, although this number included many "repeaters." American farms continued to offer employment to all arrivals. (Offering employment to aliens was not illegal.) For Mexican workers the formalities of legal entry could be uncertain and expensive: often illegal entry was quicker and cheaper. Growers found it profitable to hire illegals because they could save a great deal of administrative work and substantial fees. *Braceros* and "wetbacks" often worked on the same crews. Administrative processes reached the ultimate in absurdity: illegals could be transported back across the border and then readmitted as "legally contracted" workers. It was a process aptly called "drying out" the wetbacks. American agriculture needed workers: the federal government and the Mexican government could cooperate to fill that demand.

Mexican immigration on permanent visa began to increase very rapidly in the 1950s. Both permanent and temporary immigration reached a postwar peak in 1956 when there were 65,047 permanent legal immigrants. But the real drama of the decade 1950–1960 was "Operation Wetback," which repeated the great repatriation of the Depression era, but this time with emphasis upon the illegality rather than the indigence of those sent back.

Operation Wetback was conducted by the U.S. Immigration and Naturalization Service. It was organized with military precision to begin in June of 1954. California was the first target and then Texas, but the campaign was widened to include cities as far away from the border as Spokane, Chicago, Kansas City, and St. Louis.

Operation Wetback was very successful. The apprehensions reached 875,000 in fiscal 1953 and a huge 1,035,282 in 1954. In five years the astonishing total of 3.8 million illegal Mexican immigrants were found and expelled. Only 63,515 were deported in formal proceedings; the others were simply removed under threat of deportation. Most were sent not to the border, but with the cooperation of the Mexican government to points in Mexico near their original homes.

The resulting shock waves in the Mexican American communities greatly deepened the prevailing distrust and alienation. In the process there were some important infringements of civil rights. Hundreds of thousands of American citizens were stopped and queried because they "looked Mexican." In fact, if a person who "looked Mexican" could not immediately produce documentary evidence of his legal status when questioned in the street or any other public place, he ran the risk of arrest and being sent "home" to Mexico. Despite these outrages, there were nonetheless many, particularly labor leaders, who saw virtually unrestrained immigration as damaging. Mexican American spokesmen themselves were beginning to feel that a continuously supplied pool of wetback labor undermined any economic or social gains. There was also considerable resentment in the Mexican community about the *bracero* program.

Meanwhile the immigration people believed that the problem of the Mexican illegals had been solved (at least for the present) by the huge volume of these repatriations. (It seems likely, however, that many of the expellees simply reentered with clean papers, because the totals of legal immigration grew considerably in the following years.) However, ironically, a consequence of the repatriations was more pressure for the importation of *braceros*. Illegal aliens were no longer an effective substitute for contract labor on the ranches of the Southwest.

By 1960, sentiment against both Mexican immigrants and Mexican contract laborers had hardened considerably. Congress listened more attentively to labor interests. It is also very probable that the long decline of agricultural power in the Border States meant that agriculture no longer dominated legislative opinion. Whatever the reason for the change in attitude, any reasonable future projection of the 1960 to 1963 immigration totals was frightening to Border State residents. Legally there had never been any quotas. There was, however, a convenient administrative mechanism available in the Act of 1952. Acccordingly on July 1, 1963, the U.S. Department of Labor announced simply that any job offer to a potential Mexican immigrant would have to be certified by the department. In turn, the department required verification from state employment agencies. No Mexican could take a job that would adversely affect domestic wages and working conditions or one that had domestic applicants.

The same slow reversal of public opinion had yet other important consequences. First, the *bracero* program was halted (with some minor exceptions) at the end of 1964. The next year Congress imposed a ceiling of 120,000 immigrants a year from all Western Hemisphere countries, to become effective in 1968. This created a new and unprecedented atmosphere of control: the "close and friendly" border had disappeared, perhaps forever.

WHO WERE THE MEXICAN IMMIGRANTS?

Immigration statistics offer only a crude profile of the immigrants, but it is possible to make some important comparisons. We know that the Mexican immigrants tend to have been even younger, less skilled, and less well educated than other immigrants. They have been predominantly male. (Exceptions are few: in the last few years, with job certification controls, the profile has shifted a bit to include more professionals and more wives and children.)

In earlier years the American economy could easily use such immigrants; those coming from Europe included a large proportion in occupations requiring little training. Unskilled Italians, Poles, Scandinavians, and Irish were absorbed by construction and other industries needing a great deal of labor. However, such opportunities have rapidly declined, even in the relatively underdeveloped Border States.

Over the years there have also been important changes in the announced destinations of the new Mexican arrivals, some of great significance. Typically the immigrant of earlier years was bound for a company town, an agricultural work camp, or perhaps an urban enclave somewhere in the Border States: from 1910 to 1929 Texas was the most popular destination. Slowly California became more attractive, and figures from 1960 to 1964 show an impressive 55.7 percent going to California and only 25.1 percent to Texas. Arizona took 5.7 percent and New Mexico 2.5 percent. Areas outside the Border States have never interested many Mexicans. Only 10.6 percent in this period intended to go beyond this very limited part of the United States. These shifts in distribution of the immigrants (as well as the shifting proportions of the foreign-born within each state) greatly affect life opportunities in all Mexican-American communities.

Whatever their destination, it seems that the rural population of inland Mexico was the main source—either directly, or by way of an earlier and not satisfactory move to one of Mexico's larger cities. The most important single geographic source is probably the great Mesa Central, a large plateau area in central Mexico far from the U.S. border which contains, as it happens, a great many of Mexico's most acute social problems. Most Mexicans who wanted to leave Mexico tended to be impoverished and unskilled. There have always been many such persons in Mexico, and Mexican economic growth has seemed ironically to mean that her lower-class groups are getting an even smaller share of the total national income of Mexico. The real question about Mexican immigration is not why so many Mexicans came to the United States, but why so few?

Leo Grebler suggests that much of the ebb and flow of Mexican immigration can be explained by four factors. First, the urge to immigrate simply lay dormant until the Mexican revolution released masses of agricultural peons. Second, alternative methods of immigration were nearly always available. An increase or decrease in the number of recruited contract workers often meant a corresponding increase or decrease in permanent immigration. Third, changes in the volume of Mexican immigration tend to be related to business cycles in the United States. Fourth, administrative controls affected the movements. The real force at all times, Grebler concludes, was a "persistent disparity in per-capita real income, together with a highly and perhaps even increasingly uneven distribution of income in Mexico itself." [11]

LAWS, COURTS, AND IMMIGRANTS

Before 1875 there were no federal statutes in the United States regulating immigration.[12] Two concepts determined this policy of presenting an "open door" to all the world. It was felt that America was to be an asylum and a place of opportunity for Europe's "downtrodden masses." It was also widely believed that any mixture of nationalities that would enter this country could be "melted" into American life. Both these ideals —and a practical need for unskilled labor in American industry and agriculture—had to be faced down in Congress before there could be any restrictions on immigration.

However, Congress could and did control the quality of the immigrants. Qualitative restrictions appeared as early as 1875, and the list of aliens excludable for physical or moral reasons grew with each revision of the laws governing immigration. There were specific acts against Chinese immigrants in 1882 and against alien contract labor in both 1885 and 1891, although neither much affected Mexican immigration. These dilutions in practice of the traditional American welcome were based on a feeling that the newer immigrants were "less American" than the older. Americans began to feel more receptive to racist ideology. Large-scale importations of unskilled labor were less needed in the late nineteenth century in every part of the nation except in the Border States. Further, the nation suffered a series of acute agricultural and financial depressions that created much domestic unemployment. In Congress the debates about immigration reflected a new and tough nationalism quite typical of the early twentieth century. And although Mexican immigration did not yet figure importantly in the debates, the new feeling did lead directly to the Quota Law of 1921 and thus to the first overall control of the *number* of immigrants attempted in this country. The Quota Law was revised in 1924 and became the basis of all future immigration policy.

---

[11] Grebler, *Mexican Immigration,* p. 93.
[12] This study of federal laws and Mexican immigration is based on a section by Ronald Wyse in Grebler, *Mexican Immigration.*

Not until later did Mexican immigration become a subject for national debate. The qualitative restrictions of 1917 were a reaction to the large numbers of immigrants coming not from Mexico but from southern and eastern Europe. Mexicans were exempt from the quantitative controls imposed in 1921 and 1924, as were all Western Hemisphere countries. In Congress the exemption was justified on the basis of "pan-Americanism" as a principle and traditional policy. There were, as yet, comparatively few immigrants from either Mexico or Canada and it was easy for Congress to be a "good neighbor." Nonetheless the idea of both qualitative and quantitative controls over immigration had been established by 1924. The actual mechanism of exclusion was available for use when needed.

By 1926 a great increase in Mexican immigration encouraged the Congressional restrictionists to make a strong drive to "close the back door." The racial argument against Mexicans appeared again. As Congressman John Box of Texas put it, Mexicans were "illiterate, unclean, peonized masses" and racially speaking, he felt they were a "mixture of Mediterranean-blooded Spanish peasants with low grade Indians who did not fight to extinction but submitted and multiplied as serfs." [13] But the restrictionists overreached themselves. If they excluded only Mexicans they would anger powerful economic interests. If they excluded all Western Hemisphere nationals, they would have a difficult time applying the policy to Canadians. Moreover, there was always the danger that the Republic of Mexico might be offended. But, in fact, no new legislation was needed. Merely enforcing the qualitative provisions would achieve the desired effect. Accordingly, in 1929, consular officers in Mexico began to turn down applicants for legal admission on the grounds they were likely to become "a public charge" in the United States. Thus Congress could be persuaded that no unseemly anti-Mexican legislation was needed.

The Depression era and the rise of fascism and communism in Europe brought a new concern with national security. By 1950 a substantial overgrowth of modifications and exceptions meant that the basic immigration law needed rewriting. The result was the famous McCarran-Walter Immigration and Nationality Act of 1952. Fundamentally, it recodified and retained the national origins quota system. Subsequent legislation as late as 1965 would do nothing more than modify certain particularly harsh provisions of the McCarran-Walter Act.

All of the basic laws concerning immigration left loopholes to allow importation of Mexican workers even when the main purpose of the laws seemed to be to restrict such importation. The Immigration Act of 1917 and the McCarran-Walter Act both contain such exceptions and

[13] Quoted in Grebler, *Mexican Immigration*, p. D-10.

provide for a fully developed administrative apparatus to control the flow of workers. Whatever the intent of Congress, the loopholes could always be opened or closed administratively.

One excellent example of such a loophole is the continuous admission of Mexican workers as "commuter" workers. Under the Quota Law of 1924, a Mexican "immigrant" who qualified for immigration could be issued a card which permitted him to enter the United States every day to work in Border State cities and then return home to Mexico at night.

Mexican contract labor has entered continuously under a series of complicated special laws and agreements in addition to loophole provisions of both the Quota Law of 1917 and the McCarran-Walter Act. Sometimes the importations were made under joint control of the United States and Mexico and sometimes not. When Congress passed Public Law 78 in July of 1951 allowing the *braceros,* strong governmental controls became effective for the first time. Notable among the controls were two laws that made the illegal smuggling of aliens a felony and gave federal officials the right to patrol private lands within 25 miles of the United States-Mexico border.

A considerable body of administrative law affects Mexican immigrants although it is much too complicated to sketch here.[14] Most of this regulation was created by the Immigration and Naturalization Service (of the U.S. Department of Justice) and by a series of judicial decisions on the nature of American citizenship. The growth and administration of this law is a story in itself and sometimes not very pretty. The Service has not always observed either its own regulations or the ordinary civil rights of the citizens and aliens affected. (A U.S. Supreme Court decision in 1886 established that the "person" in the Fifth Amendment guarantee of due process of law includes not just citizens and nationals of the United States but also resident aliens.) Nor does the Mexican American population, alien and non-alien, regard *la migra* (a nickname for the Immigration Service officers) with any feeling except varying degrees of resentment. Service regulations often were invoked in punitive and arbitrary fashion by employers and local authorities throughout the Border States. In theory, of course, there was always recourse to the courts, but such alternatives were for the wealthy, not for poor and ill-informed Mexican immigrants.

In recent years the Mexican American population has been profoundly affected by a series of judicial decisions regarding the "dual national." In fact, much of the current legal doctrine on loss of nationality stems from decisions affecting Mexican immigrants. These decisions

---

[14] For a short but excellent summary, see Ronald Wyse in Grebler, *Mexican Immigration,* p. D-19.

were a direct result of the heavy illegal immigration and the equally massive repatriations of Mexicans. Legally speaking, children born to Mexican contract laborers (or even to illegal aliens) are American citizens who hold "dual nationality." Thus many U.S. citizens were illegally repatriated to Mexico. Many then endangered their U.S. citizenship by voting in a Mexican election or by serving in the Mexican army. Without going into the details, the general effect of the judicial decisions is that a "dual national" Mexican, although residing in Mexico, has no special handicaps in U.S. citizenship. If he wishes to renounce his allegiance to the United States, he must do so formally and at a mature age.

Ultimately the right to vote and, to some degree, acceptance by the larger American society depends upon citizenship, which is normally acquired through naturalization. Mexicans have been extraordinarily slow to become naturalized. Between 1959 and 1966 only 2.4 percent to 5 percent of the eligible Mexicans became citizens each year. Other immigrants entering at the same time with the same length of residence naturalized at a rate of between 23 percent and 33 percent.[15]

None of the explanations advanced for this low rate of naturalization is conclusive. A low rate is consistent with the social isolation of Mexican Americans. In earlier years the Mexican consuls made a deliberate effort to promote loyalty to the homeland. Mexicans have mistrusted U.S. governmental authority, and many Mexicans did not intend to remain permanently in the United States. Finally, the generally low economic and educational level of the immigrants has made naturalization more difficult than for other immigrant groups. Illiteracy rates are very much higher in Mexico than in any European country.

THE NEW BORDER

A number of powerful interests worked together to tighten the border gradually. Probably the slow erosion of political power suffered by the railroads, the great ranches, and the mining interests of the Border States is the single most critical factor. Also important in the debate were northeastern businessmen who saw no reason for supplying cheap labor to their southwestern competitors, along with state and local welfare agencies, and organized labor. These forces dominated Congressional debate on the Immigration and Nationality Act of 1965. It is very likely that these same forces will continue to oppose any relaxation of its application.

This bill was designed by a pro-labor administration to eliminate

[15] See Leo Grebler, "The Naturalization of Mexican Immigrants in the United States," *The International Migration Review,* I (Fall, 1966), 17–32.

the national origins quotas embodied in the McCarran-Walter Act. The original form of the new bill would have left Western Hemisphere provisions almost unchanged. But in the House and Senate hearings, the Western Hemisphere unexpectedly became the main concern. The bill was amended to allow no more than 120,000 persons per year from the New World countries. To soften its impact, the ceiling would not take effect until 1968 and not until a final deliberation from a special commission on Western Hemisphere immigration. The legislative background of the Act of 1965 was such that the advocates of removing the origins quotas for Europe could achieve their goal only by accepting a quota in the Western Hemisphere. Republican restrictionist sentiment was alarmed by a sharp new rise in immigration, particularly from the Caribbean area. The compromise, in fact, was possible only because it seemed that the job certification procedure was holding down Mexican immigration anyway. Something of the embarrassment for Mexico was removed by making similar certification procedures apply to all Western Hemisphere countries.

According to this law, immediate relatives of earlier immigrants are in a preferred category without reference to either quota or job skills. This provision has meant changes in the characteristics of immigrants. Only 32,967 Mexicans entered in 1964. The total rose to 37,969 in 1965 and 45,163 in 1966, and the proportion of housewives and children reached 78.1 percent for 1965–1966. This is an important increase over earlier averages in which the proportion of housewives and children ran as low as 50.1 percent (1955–1959). There appears to be a heavy backlog of relatives in categories not subject to any quota; there is also some evidence that the "migration potential" is building up in Mexico. Grebler quotes a report from the Border Patrol covering the 48-county area north of Kern County in California. It shows that the number of illegal Mexican immigrants apprehended doubled in the first seven months of 1965 against the first seven months of 1964.[16]

The new restrictions will have profound long-range effects on the Mexican minority, some of which can be inferred from the present condition of the Mexican Americans. This condition will be described in detail in later chapters. Other effects are not easy to anticipate. Meanwhile the current internal migration from Texas to California will probably continue to supply California urban centers with a large number of rural laborers. It should be emphasized that in nearly every respect those

---

[16] Official statistics from the Service about the apprehension of illegal immigrants may reflect increased efficiency or increased illegal immigration. It is evident that any important reported increase in illegal entry reflcts on Border Patrol efficiency. Generally the border is more efficiently watched now than in earlier years. It is probably safe to assume that fewer illegals enter, assuming no change in the "immigration potential."

arrivals from rural American areas are as impoverished and as unacculturated as are immigrants from Mexico.

Generally we can guess that there will be more pressure to plug the administrative loophole that allows the "green carders" to work in this country. Labor-intensive Border State industries (most notably the agriculture of Texas and California) will be forced into increasingly rapid mechanization, thus accelerating Mexican migration to the cities. Industries that have depended upon non-unionized, cheap Mexican labor will probably face a new wave of union activity. In general, Mexican Americans should be able to make economic gains and these gains will be shared with nonwhite minority groups of the Border States, most notably the Negroes. But none of these changes will appear dramatically or soon. The urban Mexican American communities will for many years contain a huge reservoir of unskilled, uneducated migrants from the rural areas of the Border States and Mexico.

Without further adventures in prognosis, we may now point out that "the close and friendly" border is tighter and less friendly than before. Perhaps, in time, as the distance in skills, education, and social status grows larger between immigrant and old resident, the Mexican American community itself may grow more restrictionist. In the past it has always been somewhat ambivalent. Higher-status Mexican Americans tended to be more restrictionist than those of lower status (except in some of the cities directly along the border). The newer generation of minority leaders recognizes the economic damage of the open border. It is also likely that the new border will affect Mexican American social stratification, both internally and in the larger society, as profoundly as it has affected everything else Mexican in the United States.

Mexican Americans as a minority group have certain demographic characteristics. These are the realities behind Mexican American social life and values. To understand the characteristics of this group, we must answer questions like the following: How many Mexican Americans live in the United States? Where do they live? How many are really "Mexican" —that is, born in Mexico? What is their position in the labor markets of the Southwest? How well are they acculturated to the norms of life in the United States? What does "poverty" mean in the Mexican-American context?

PORTRAIT OF A POPULATION

Profile

of the

Mexican

American

In 1960 there were not quite 4 million Mexican Americans living in the United States.[1] (The best available estimates for 1970 show 5,073,000 persons of Mexican descent.[2]) This is not many people in a nation of more than 200 million, but because of their concentration in an area of only five states, the Mexican Americans—the most significant minority in the region —are of great national importance. In the five states of the Southwest they were 12 percent of the roughly 29 million. By contrast, the Puerto Rican minority in the East receives much more attention and yet is much smaller, including only 873,000 persons in 1960. Even mainland Puerto Rico shelters only about half as many people as there are Mexicans in the United States. Immigrant Mexicans and their descendants now form the largest concentration of people of Latin American descent outside Latin America. Further, there is every

[1] Certain technical problems in the U.S. Census make it impossible to trace the growth of the Mexican American minority over time or to be sure of its exact numerical size within an ordinary margin of error. First, the present census category of "white persons of Spanish surname" (mostly Mexican Americans) was established only in 1950, and thus earlier figures are not comparable. Second, general changes in the definitions of "rural" and "urban" after 1940 also complicate the problem. See U.S. Census of the Population, 1960, "Persons of Spanish Surname," PC(2)1B, for an analysis of the surname definition.

[2] These estimates are reported in U.S. Department of Commerce, Bureau of the Census, *Current Population Reports, Population Characteristics,* "Spanish-American Population: November 1969," Series P–20, No. 195, February 20, 1970, p. 2.

chance that this minority will continue to grow faster than any other ethnic group in the United States.[3]

In 1960 (the census year that provides most of our information) most Mexican Americans lived in California and Texas. Each of these states had more than 1.4 million Mexican Americans, and together they held 82 percent of the entire southwestern Mexican population. Thus the three remaining states of Arizona, Colorado, and New Mexico held only 18 percent, although in all three states the Mexican Americans were the most important minority by a wide margin, considerably outnumbering the Negroes and other nonwhites (Indians and Orientals). The Los Angeles metropolitan area alone had 629,000 Mexican Americans, a concentration exceeding the total number in Arizona, Colorado, and New Mexico combined. Changes since 1960 probably have increased the proportion living in California. As a consequence, the social and economic milieu (including the degree to which the local social system accepts or rejects Mexican Americans) of just two states, Texas and California, is of critical importance to Mexican Americans.

Not all Mexicans live in the Southwest, although their failure to move any more deeply into the northwestern and midwestern states is largely unexplained. Small communities of Mexican Americans are found in all large western and midwestern urban areas, with notable but relatively small enclaves appearing in Kansas, Michigan, Wisconsin, Illinois, (especially in and around Chicago) and some other areas. However, no well-informed estimate of their numbers in 1960 is likely to exceed 13 percent of the total Mexican American population.[4]

Not only do most Mexican Americans live in California or Texas, but even inside these states they are concentrated in particular areas.[5]

[3] The Mexican American rate of increase betwen 1950 and 1960 was 4.1 percent against less than 3.1 percent for Anglo Americans, 4.0 percent for nonwhites, and 3.3 percent for the total population in the Southwest. The entire U.S. population increased by only 1.7 percent a year from 1950 to 1960.

[4] Much of this material is based on a manuscript prepared for the Mexican American Study Project at the University of California, Los Angeles, by Leo Grebler, et al, in *The Mexican American People* (New York: The Free Press, 1970).

[5] Careful studies of Mexican American population distribution show that contrary to popular belief there is not a simple relation between distribution patterns and the proximity of the counties of southwestern states to the Mexican border.

Only four counties in the Southwest hold more than 100,000 Spanish-surname persons. Three of these include major urban centers. The four counties are Los Angeles county in California and El Paso, Bexar, and Hidalgo counties in Texas. Of the four, only Hidalgo in south Texas is heavily agricultural. There are also many Mexican Americans in Cameron County, which includes the city of Brownsville. Other urban areas with high numbers of Mexican residents are Corpus Christi, Houston, Laredo, Albuquerque, Phoenix, San Diego, San Francisco, Oakland, and some parts of the southern California metropolitan complex. Certain other areas of labor-intensive irrigated agriculture also have many Mexican Americans.

Los Angeles and smaller nearby cities in southern California hold most of the California population. Southern Texas, particularly the lower Rio Grande valley and some of the large border cities, houses most of the Texas Mexican population. Laredo was 80 percent Mexican in 1960, and Tyler, in east Texas, only 1 percent Mexican. These disparities are historical and social "accidents" of considerable consequence. This population is growing at the rapid rate of 51 percent every 10 years—faster than either the dominant Anglo population (37 percent) or nonwhites (49 percent) in these states. Immigration has accounted for only some of this rapid growth. Natural population increase is far more important, as we shall see later.

Still other historical and social accidents have forced many Mexican Americans into an unusual community pattern in their areas of greatest concentration. Although the degree of actual separation from the dominant Anglo and the subordinate Negro populations varies considerably from city to city, Mexicans generally live together in distinctively "Mexican" neighborhoods. (These are frequently referred to throughout the Southwest as *barrios*. The term is roughly equivalent to "ghetto," although there is a slight difference in connotation.) It is interesting to compare the Mexican *barrio* with the more common patterns by which ethnic ghettos have been established in the U.S. Most American ethnic enclaves have been produced when a subpopulation appeared quite suddenly in a city. Classically (as with the Irish in Boston and the Negroes in Chicago) the newcomers settled in cheap housing in the older central areas of a big city. There are such Mexican enclaves in the Border States, but many of them originated quite differently from the Little Italys and Chinatowns of classic sociology, simply because Mexicans were settlers first in so many towns.

One typical town plan in the Border States was the settlement around a traditionally Mexican *plaza* (central area). When the railroads

---

State by state we find that few Mexicans live in northern California but a great many live in the southern part of the state and the lowlands of the agricultural valleys. Arizona is very sparsely populated in general and the Mexican Americans are confined to one urban area and to some irrigated valleys. In New Mexico the area of old Spanish colonization in north central New Mexico has a moderate concentration of Mexican Americans, with a strong nucleus in Albuquerque. Some population is found in the lower reaches of the Rio Grande valley, where irrigated agriculture is well developed.

West Texas is sparsely populated on the whole; a high proportion of the counties are heavily Mexican American. South Texas has large concentrations. Anglos and Negroes generally dominate the north and northeast portions of Texas. Two counties in Colorado—the urban areas of Pueblo and Denver—have a considerable number of Spanish-surname persons.

This material is based upon an unpublished study for the Mexican American Study Project (Los Angeles: University of California, December, 1967).

and highways brought quick growth of the Anglo population, such growth tended to center around the new terminals or nodes of transportation. The Mexican plaza area was bypassed and tended to deteriorate. In time, as in Albuquerque, Los Angeles, and dozens of other cities, the plaza area remained as the "Mexican Downtown" or as a carefully reconstructed and often glamorized tourist center.

Still other Mexican enclaves are the residue of early labor camps. In southern California such remnants of times past as Santa Fe Springs and Pacoima in Los Angeles county and the Casa Blanca area of Riverside are really the skeletons of old labor camps bypassed and isolated inside growing, spreading cities. Whole families of Mexicans emigrated or were imported into these camps to serve such functions as ranching, railway maintenance, citrus harvesting and packing, and brick-making. The ethnic population may remain but it ceases to be employed at its old occupation. In yet other areas the enclaves remain on the fringes of the metropolitan area and continue to serve as agricultural labor markets. The Mexican American population may then work both inside the city and outside in the fields as the season demands, as in Fresno, California. Many such settlements have disappeared; some are in the process of urban renewal; some have been overwhelmed and displaced by a rapid rise in land values.

There are also some parts of the Border States in which Mexican Americans are not found in ghettos or enclaves but rather dominate the life of the community. This pattern appears frequently in the small towns of northern New Mexico and southern Texas and also in large Texas border and near-border cities like Laredo. No other American minority shows such an extraordinary range, from highly segregated to almost completely nonsegregated living patterns.

Large numbers of Mexican Americans still live in rural areas—so many, in fact, that a prevailing American stereotype is that Mexicans are primarily a rural people. Actually, Mexicans are moving into cities (primarily into the old enclaves) at a very rapid rate, and this process, noticeable since World War II, seems to be gaining in speed. By 1960 any portrait of the American citizen of Mexican descent as an agricultural laborer or rural resident became a serious distortion. Although they did hold more than half of all agricultural labor jobs in both California and Texas, the demand for such labor is now comparatively small and shrinking so rapidly that the percentages are misleading. Machines are replacing men in American agriculture, and nowhere is this happening faster than in California and Texas, where huge and highly capitalized farms are introducing farm machinery as fast as it can be perfected. Mexican Americans, in fact, are even more likely to move into cities than are Negroes or

Anglos. Only about a fifth of each of these three groups now lives in rural areas in the Border States. Generally this move to the cities happened later with Mexican Americans than with other groups, and a bit more slowly. It is most apparent in Texas and in California.

The importance of this rapid urbanization cannot be overemphasized. Between 1950 and 1960 the Mexican American rural population of the Southwest fell only slightly in absolute numbers, but the loss in certain areas was so large (23 percent in New Mexico rural areas, 17 percent in Colorado) that many highly traditional and isolated towns in the northern section of New Mexico became ghost villages. Large numbers of the younger people moved to Albuquerque and to other states, notably California. These rural losses are noticeable in all states except California.

The nativity patterns of Mexican Americans are also changing, although not so dramatically as their settlement patterns. In the nineteenth century, most Mexican Americans were U.S. citizens: they became so by treaty in 1848. Then the great waves of immigration in the early part of the twentieth century tipped the scales toward the foreign-born. (See Chapter Three.) Since then, the proportion of native-born has been increasing slowly until in 1960 85 percent of Mexican Americans were born in the United States. As immigration becomes increasingly restricted (apparently the pattern of the future) we can expect the proportion of native-born to increase.

There are some important differences between the nativity classes or "generations." [6] (For a rough notion of their relative importance in the population, it is sufficient to note that the third generation formed 55 percent of the 1960 total, the second generation formed 30 percent, and the first generation or foreign-born formed 15 percent. Proportions differ greatly from area to area: third generation persons, for example, were heavily concentrated in New Mexico. Thus the overall figures may be misleading in any given area. (We discuss this interaction between nativity and locality in Chapter Seven.) In general the differences between the generations follow the patterns one might anticipate from other immigrant populations: third or later generation Mexican Americans generally tend to be better educated and to make more money than the foreign-born, but strangely they do not receive higher incomes than do the second generation. Generally, the third generation tend to have more stable families.[7] They are also more likely to remarry once divorced or

6 Throughout this volume we shall define "generation" as follows: for the census designation "native born of native parents," we shall use the term "third generation"; for the census designation "native born of foreign or mixed parentage" we shall use "second generation." For "foreign born" we shall use "first generation."

7 In 1960, foreign born Mexicans were far more likely to have families headed by a female or a male other than the husband-father. Despite this fact, reported divorce

deserted, to intermarry with native Americans more frequently, to obtain more schooling, and in most instances to exhibit the signs of a group achieving some degree of penetration into the larger society. They are, for example, less overrepresented in the low-skilled manual occupations than the foreign-born and have begun to move into white collar occupations. Leo Grebler remarks that the most significant contrast in economic standing is between the first and the second generation. Native parentage seems to carry few additional benefits. He suggests, therefore, that in contrast to most other minorities (excluding the Negro) more than three generations may be necessary for Mexican immigrants to approximate the income position of the general southwestern population.

The median age of Mexican Americans is low: 19.6 years. The median age of the third generation was even lower, only 13 years. This age structure is the result of an exceptionally high birth rate. Using as a measure the number of children ever born per 1,000 women ever married, the great difference between Mexican and Anglo fertility begins in the 15- to 19-year-old age group. The fertility difference increases with every age group thereafter. The young Mexican American women are 41 percent more fertile than Anglos of the same age, and by ages 45–49 (when most Anglo women stop having children) Mexican American women are 107 percent more fertile.

As one might expect from the high fertility rates, Mexican American families are extremely large. They are so large, in fact, as to make Mexican participation in the ordinary material rewards of American life much more marginal than that of most other populations identified by the census. No other category of people in the United States except the American Indian matches or approximates the typical Mexican American family size of 4.8 persons. Southwestern Anglos, for comparison, averaged 3.4 persons per family in 1960 and the nonwhites in the same region, 4.5 persons.

These and other age disproportions between urban Anglo Americans and urban Mexican Americans show clearly in the age pyramids in Figure 3–1. The median age of the entire Mexican population, 19.6 in 1960, was a full 10 years lower than that of Anglos and 4 years lower than that of nonwhites. More than 40 percent of the Mexican Americans were children of less than 15 years of age. By contrast, only about 30 percent of the Anglo population was less than 15 years old.

Thus the 1,500,000 Mexican children is the Southwest are an enor-

---

and separation rates do not differ by nativity. This may be because the Mexican-born men have died, and/or because the women who have been deserted or divorced conceal what they define as embarrassing information from the census taker.

FIGURE 4–1

AGE PYRAMIDS FOR URBAN ANGLO AND SPANISH-SURNAME
POPULATION IN THE SOUTHWEST, 1960

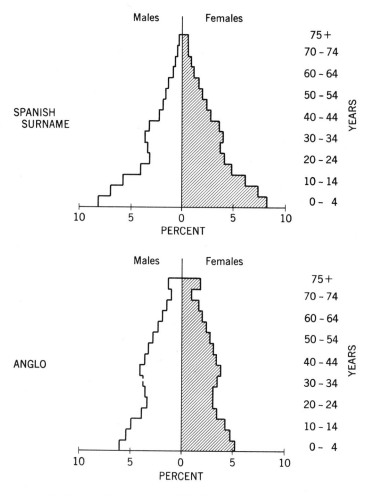

Source: U.S. Census of Population, 1960, Vol. 1, Parts 4, 6, 7, 33, 45, Table
96: PC (2) 1B, Table 2. Compiled by Mexican American Study Project (Los
Angeles: University of California, 1966).

mous 16 percent of all the children in these states. The ratio of Mexicans
to Anglos, without respect to age, is about one to seven. The child ratio
is about one to five. Thus the impact on the school system and other
youth-serving agencies is far greater than overall population ratios would
indicate.

These very large and very young families portend some definite trends for the future. First, the capacity of the school systems of the Border States to respond to their needs will be increasingly tested. Second, the large number of children implies a high rate of future population growth. Third, Mexican acceptance or rejection of current ideas on birth control are of special significance. Recent survey data indicate that Mexican Americans are at least as willing as other Americans to accept the propriety of birth control.[8] This is especially true for younger persons.

The dependency ratio in Mexican American families (a statistical relationship between those who by age are likely to work and those who are not likely to work) is higher than for either Anglos or nonwhites. In the Southwest as a whole there were 121 dependents in 1960 for every 100 Mexican Americans 20 to 64 years old. There were 85 dependents for every 100 Anglos in the same age range and 98 dependents for every 100 nonwhites of comparable age. Of all five states of the Southwest, California has the most favorable dependency ratio and Colorado the least favorable. The high Mexican dependency ratio is due almost entirely to the large number of dependent young people. There were comparatively few old people in 1960. Dependency ratios run the highest in rural non-farm areas where the child population is the highest. Thus the ratios considerably magnify regional and local differences in the socioeconomic status of the Mexicans.

But, of course, dependency ratios are not the whole story. Mexican families also suffer disproportionately from high separation rates (without divorce)—far more than might be expected from the traditional stereotype of the strong Mexican family. "Broken families"—that is, families headed by persons other than the husband and wife—reached 16 percent in 1960, a figure much larger than for Anglos. The percentage of separated and divorced women is somewhat larger than among the Anglo population, although smaller than among southwestern nonwhites.

America's Mexican minority is distinctive also in its sex ratio. Generally there are more males than females, in contrast to the ratio in all other population groups in the Southwest. In rural nonfarm areas the disproportion is very great. Nearly all of this difference is the result of the importation of *braceros* from Mexico. As noted earlier, the program ended after the 1960 census. In cities the excess of males still holds, although less sharply than in rural areas. Even the older age groups have men and women in about equal numbers, in marked contrast to the rest of the U.S. population, in which women outnumber men.

8 Surveys in Los Angeles and San Antonio relate to attitudes. See Grebler, *et al, The Mexican American People.*

TO EARN A LIVING

These patterns, quite different from those of the dominant Anglo American population, profoundly affect the share of income available to each Mexican American individual. Except for the relatively small Indian group, no population in the Southwest is so severely pinched economically. The Mexican head of a family must make his lower income stretch to cover a larger household. The chances of his earning a livable wage are low and are not increasing rapidly; nor are they proportionately increased by education. They also vary greatly from state to state and even from city to city throughout the Southwest. The magnitude of the difference between Mexican and Anglo is indicated by the fact that in 1960 Mexican Americans earned only $.47 per person for every dollar of Anglo income earned per person. This was a return per person lower than even that of nonwhites.[9]

To examine the critical factors of income more closely: in 1959 the median income of all Mexican American males in the Southwest was $2,768. This is only 57 percent of the median earned by an Anglo male in the same area. Further, when older males in both groups are compared, relative Mexican income declines steadily. Mexicans have not had job mobility, and foreign-born immigrants form a larger percentage of older age groups than they do of younger ones. Median income differences between states are enormous, ranging from $5,533 in California to $2,914 in Texas. The Anglo median income in Texas is twice that of comparable Mexicans. Texas nonwhites, mostly Negroes, earn $2,591 or only slightly less than Mexicans. Other states range in between.

In summary: about 35 percent of the Spanish-surname families fell below the "poverty line" of $3,000 annual income,[10] although they were less than 10 percent of all families in the Southwest.

Their tiny share of southwestern income cannot be ascribed entirely to lack of education. Income differences, on the contrary, tend to *widen* as educational attainment increases. Nor does Mexican income show the

[9] For a careful survey of this dilution of Mexican American income by large families, see Frank G. Mittelbach and Grace Marshall, *The Burden of Poverty*, Advance Report 5 (Los Angeles: University of California, Mexican-American Study Project, 1966).

[10] Much of this material is based on an analysis of income and occupational data prepared by Walter Fogel and Leo Grebler in *The Mexican American People*. The data also appear in Walter Fogel, *Mexican Americans in Southwest Labor Markets*, Advance Report 10 (Los Angeles: University of California, Mexican American Study Project, 1967).

A family income of $3,000 per year is widely used as a statistical "poverty line" definition. The President's Council of Economic Advisers adopted it in 1964 and simultaneously adopted $1,500 as the "poverty line" for individuals not living in families. Mittelbach and Marshall, *The Burden of Poverty*, p. 13.

same patterns by age as in the Anglo population: Mexican income does not tend to increase as much toward middle age as it does among Anglos.

Nonetheless there are some hopeful signs. The most important is simply the fact that the median income of Mexican American individuals in the Southwest is increasing. There is some moderate upgrading in the Mexican American occupational profile in both California and Texas. Some of these changes were produced by migration to California where all incomes tend to be higher, from Texas and other southwestern states. Another encouraging factor is the increase in the percentage of native-born Mexicans. In any case, as Walter Fogel concludes, "the gap between the minority and the majority has not widened." This is particularly important because these gains occurred despite the influx of more than 293,000 immigrants in the 1950s.

TABLE 4-1

OCCUPATIONAL DISTRIBUTION OF URBAN MALES,
BY ETHNIC GROUP, 1960

Occupational Category	Anglo	Spanish-Surname	Nonwhite
Professionals	15.1	4.6	6.1
Managers and Proprietors	14.7	4.9	3.6
Clerical Workers	7.8	5.5	6.1
Sales Workers	9.2	4.1	2.3
Craftsmen	21.5	18.2	10.8
Operatives	15.8	25.4	20.0
Private Household Workers	0.1	0.1	0.9
Service Workers, except Private Household	5.4	8.4	18.6
Laborers	4.4	15.8	18.3
Farm Laborers	0.6	7.3	2.1
Farm Managers	0.7	0.6	1.9
Occupation not reported	4.7	5.1	9.3

Source: U.S. Census of Population. 1960, Vol. I, Parts 4, 6, 7, 33, and 45. Table 58; and PC(2) 1B, Table 6. Compiled by Mexican American Study Project (Los Angeles: University of California, 1966).

Income directly reflects the occupational position of the southwestern Mexican. In nearly all of the broad occupational classifications used by the census, Mexicans held poorer jobs paying less money than did native American whites. (See Table 4–1.) Most urban Mexican males are employed as semiskilled workers and laborers. In 1960, only 19 percent compared to nearly half of the Anglos worked in white collar occupations (professional, managerial, clerical, and sales). The occupational structures of the employed nonwhite and the employed Mexican American, however, are very similar except that the nonwhites get less craft work and more service work.

A true picture of Mexican participation in the labor market does not emerge until the broad classifications and certain important trends in the American labor market are examined closely. First, Mexicans hold the poorer jobs inside most broad occupational classifications. Professional and technical job holders, for example, are far more likely to be medical technologists than surgeons; draftsmen than architects; social workers than lawyers. In the managerial classification there are far more managers of small marginal restaurants than corporate executives. Further, Mexican Americans in the managerial category are far more heavily concentrated among the self-employed than among the salaried. Inside the "craft and operative" classification, Mexican participation appears nearly equal to that of Anglos in California, though not in Texas. But this broad generalization conceals the important fact that Mexicans hold the poorer jobs. In both California and Texas they are greatly underrepresented in the highly unionized and better paying jobs. Further, they hold fewer jobs in high-wage industries (aircraft, paper, chemicals, and petroleum). As operatives Mexican Americans tend to work in the furniture, apparel, and textile industries, which pay relatively low wages, and in stone, clay, and glass products manufacture. Relatively large numbers of Mexican Americans tend to work in the low wage jobs. Among service workers Mexicans do very poorly—largely because of their widespread exclusion from the city fire and police protection jobs, which pay well. This is much more true in Texas than in California (the same exclusion also hurts Negroes).

Second, a more refined analysis by Walter Fogel shows that even if the representation were equal, Mexicans would still get lower pay than Anglos for similar kinds of work. The poorest relative earnings were found among managers and sales workers—a gap in pay readily explained by the large amount of managerial self-employment. Half of all the Mexican-American managers in both Los Angeles and San Antonio were self-employed. Only a third of the Anglo managers in these two cities were self-employed.

Third, unrealistic standards keep Mexicans out of many jobs for which they are qualified. Apparently employers (and unions) often use educational attainment in hiring for many jobs in the unskilled and semiskilled occupations, although the years of formal schooling may be quite valueless to the employer. Education thus used to sort out job applicants is an important argument for some standardization or regulation in hiring procedures. Only in unskilled laborer jobs does Mexican American employment not differ in earnings from the Anglos'.

Fourth, jobs that depend entirely upon the Mexican American community bring very low comparative wages. This is, again, more true in

Texas than in California, possibly reflecting the greater isolation of the Texas Mexicans. The idea of self-sufficiency inside a ghetto community has won some attention among all U.S. minorities; but it is highly probable that Mexicans would gain more by free access to the general labor market than by self-help attempts to strengthen the Mexican American economic community.

As Fogel summarizes, "In this naive view, ethnic dependence in employment, business establishments, the professions, and capital formation is expected to raise the material welfare of the minority faster than its present dependence on the majority. Ignoring other aspects of the proposition (especially the crucial matter of capital), the evidence on relative earnings, although not entirely clearcut, serves to show its fallacy." [11]

Fifth, wage standardization is associated with high relative earnings for Mexican workers. This is generally true in California; it is somewhat less true in Texas. Standardized wages, however, nearly always imply a set of formal requirements or tests, and these requirements are likely to make entry harder for qualified Mexican Americans than for other workers. Jobs in civil service are prime examples; they carry requirements of language fluency, citizenship, and formal schooling. This problem for the "educational minority" is increasingly serious for all ethnic groups, not just Mexicans. Mexican Americans will do better when wage standardization is achieved by unionization, government legislation, or industrial concentration; but they may, as a consequence, "slip down" into unstructured labor markets, thus increasing unemployment in the lower wage market and further depressing wages. Wage standardization is particularly unfair to new immigrants from Mexico. Widespread standardization may, in time, make it difficult or very nearly impossible for a generation of immigrants to achieve any occupational progress whatever.

But these are fine points. It is perfectly obvious from the most superficial examination of the data that in general Mexican Americans hold the less desirable jobs in the Southwest because of lack of education, lack of business capital, cultural dissimilarity to the majority, and their obvious role as a low-prestige group. Further, Mexicans are disproportionately forced to work in low-wage or marginal firms—in the less profitable, nonunionized fringes of the high-wage industries. Low job earnings are also associated with the concentration of Mexicans in certain low-wage geographical areas, the lower Rio Grande valley of Texas being an example. (Of course, such areas are "low-wage" partly *because* they are heavily Mexican.)

Mexican Americans tend to work fewer weeks per year than do Anglos. This underemployment is probably a direct consequence of a

11 Fogel, *Mexican Americans in Southwest Labor Markets.*

concentration in agricultural work and of the marginality of the companies by which they are heavily employed. (The same effect seems to hurt nonwhites even more than Mexicans.) There is no evidence, however, that Mexicans are any less productive on the job than Anglos. On the other hand, it is very plain that the southwestern labor market reflects fairly substantial discrimination, however it may be disguised.

Unemployment rates for Mexicans were very high in 1960, roughly twice those for Anglos of comparable ages. For urban Mexican women the rate is even higher than for nonwhite women. Mexican unemployment tends to increase rapidly among older men and older women—even more so than for Anglos and nonwhites. Unemployment rates for teenagers are extremely high, indicating probably that the labor market is nearly as unreceptive to Mexican-American youngsters as to Negro young people. The statistics also show that women easily find work as household servants and continue to work into advanced years as do many nonwhites, in spite of the homemaking role prescribed for women by Mexican culture.

Arizona and California have the lowest rates of Mexican unemployment; Texas, the highest. A large supply of unskilled labor (from immigration, natural increase, and the "green card" commuters) is concentrated in south Texas. Here employment opportunities have not kept pace with the population. Even with a high rate of economic growth there is no prospect for any important improvement in the labor market situation in Texas. In the Southwest in general, although Mexicans are leaving rural areas, they are taking a greater share of the unskilled farm and farm laborer jobs by default. Increasingly, also, they take larger shares of nonfarm laboring jobs. This latter trend will probably continue.

Nor are many Mexicans successful entrepreneurs, even inside their own ethnic communities. Historically such ventures can be routes of progress for immigrant groups even though the individuals lack formal qualifications for many other occupations. Generally Mexican business firms are small. Even the small insurance, banking, and manufacturing interests long associated with the Negro community are largely missing among Mexicans. In Los Angeles, for instance, the Spanish-surname population of nearly 630,000 had no life insurance company even by 1960, no important manufacturers, and only one Mexican-centered savings and loan company. Fogel notes that the more wealthy persons in the Mexican community, in fact, tend to be professionals who are in business part time and rely on investments for income. Thus the original capital is founded not upon entrepreneurship but upon professional skills. Not only is the Mexican American community remarkably slow in accumulating the essential capital, but there is some evidence that the few relatively wealthy people in the community tend to "disappear" into the Anglo community. This lack of interest in community investment may, of course, explain the inability of the community to find starting investments.

TO GAIN AN EDUCATION

Mexican educational accomplishment offers very little hope for those who suggest that southwestern schools will shortly be able to end the Mexicans' labor market handicaps.[12] Some of these results are the natural consequence of several generations of *de jure* and *de facto* segregations; others simply reflect inept if not downright bad teaching. (See Chapter Five.) American schools must be judged by their output, not their intentions. By any standard other than those of rural schools in underdeveloped countries, the output for Mexican Americans is very poor.

Throughout the Southwest the Mexican American adult population was too badly educated in 1960 to participate effectively in modern American society.[13] As shown in Table 4–2, they attained a median of 7.1 years of schooling as compared with 12.1 for Anglos and 9.0 for nonwhites (adults of 25 years and over). In California the figure was highest, 8.6 years. It is lowest in Texas at 4.8 years or only slightly better than functional illiteracy.[14] In all states Negroes are better educated than Mexican Americans. (Nonwhite medians are pulled down in New Mexico and Arizona by the large proportion of Indians with extremely low levels of schooling.) Among Mexicans the incidence of functional illiteracy (0 to 4 years of elementary school) is seven times that of the Anglo population and nearly twice that of nonwhites as a whole.[15]

There seems to have been some improvement over time, particularly in urban areas. Median school years completed rose from 5.4 years in 1950 to 7.1 years. The percentage gap was thereby reduced from 52 percent to 41 percent, comparing Mexicans and Anglos throughout the five Border States. The 1960 gap is smaller when only a young group is examined: in the case of people aged 14 to 24 years the median years of school completed rise to 9.2. But this is still less than the schooling

[12] The complex relationships between income and education are explored in Walter Fogel, *Education and Income of Mexican Americans in the Southwest,* Advance Report 1 (Los Angeles: University of California, Mexican American Study Project, 1965).

[13] No figures are available before 1950, although Walter Fogel quotes an early study which estimates that not much more than a third of the Mexican American population aged 6 to 20 years were enrolled in school. By comparison, 58 percent of native white Americans were enrolled. Fogel, *Education and Income,* p. 30.

[14] Much of this chapter draws on material from Leo Grebler, *The Schooling Gap: Signs of Progress,* Advanced Report 7 (Los Angeles: University of California, Mexican American Study Project, 1967).

[15] Grebler, *The Schooling Gap,* p. 13.

TABLE 4–2

MEDIAN YEARS OF SCHOOL COMPLETED BY PERSONS
25 YEARS AND OVER, BY ETHNIC GROUP,
FIVE SOUTHWEST STATES, 1950 AND 1960

State and Population Group	Median Years Completed 1950	Median Years Completed 1960	Schooling Gap 1950 Years [a]	Schooling Gap 1950 Per Cent [b]	Schooling Gap 1960 Years [a]	Schooling Gap 1960 Per Cent [b]
Southwest, total	10.6	11.6	—	––	—	—
Anglo	11.3	12.1	—	—	—	—
Nonwhite	7.8	9.0	3.5	31	3.1	26
Spanish-surname	5.4	7.1	5.9	52	5.0	41
Arizona, total	10.0	11.2	—	—	—	—
Anglo	11.6	12.1	—	—	—	—
Nonwhite	5.5	7.0	6.1	53	5.1	42
Spanish-surname	6.0	7.0	5.6	48	5.1	42
California, total	11.6	12.1	—	—	—	—
Anglo	12.0	12.2	—	—	—	—
Nonwhite	8.9	10.6	3.1	26	1.6	13
Spanish-surname	7.8	8.6	4.2	35	3.6	30
Colorado, total	10.9	12.1	—	—	—	—
Anglo	11.3	12.2	—	—	—	—
Nonwhite	9.8	11.2	1.5	13	1.0	8
Spanish-surname	6.5	8.2	4.8	42	4.0	33
New Mexico, total	9.3	11.2	—	—	—	—
Anglo	11.8	12.2	—	—	—	—
Nonwhite	5.8	7.1	6.0	51	5.1	42
Spanish-surname	6.1	7.4	5.7	48	4.8	40
Texas, total	9.3	10.4	—	—	—	—
Anglo	10.3	11.5	—	—	—	—
Nonwhite	7.0	8.1	3.3	32	3.4	30
Spanish-surname	3.5	4.8	6.8	66	6.7	58

Source: U.S. Census of Population, 1960, State Volumes, Tables 47 and 103 and PC(2)1B, Tables 3 and 7. Table from Leo Grebler, *The Schooling Gap: Signs of Progress* (Los Angeles: University of California, Mexican American Study Project, 1967).

[a] Difference between Anglo and nonwhite or Spanish-surname median years, respectively.

[b] Difference as explained in note (a) computed as a per cent of Anglo median years, i.e., the percentage by which the Spanish-surname or nonwhite number of years falls below the Anglo figure. This calculation is added to provide a common measurement. For example, a difference of three years is equivalent to one-third if the Anglo median is 9 years but to one-fourth if the Anglo median is 12 years. Percentages are rounded.

attained by Anglos, Negroes or Orientals of the same age in the region. Furthermore, these crude measures of education (years completed) do not measure the quality of the education. These years of education probably were obtained disproportionately in rural, small town, and other schools of inferior quality.

No single measure so eloquently shows the diversity of opportunity for Mexicans as school attainment in individual cities throughout the Southwest (Table 4–3). In Lubbock, Texas, as late as 1960 the median attainment was only 3.1 years—less than half that of Negroes in the same city and barely a quarter of the 12.1 years achieved by Anglos throughout the Southwest. In Colorado Springs, Colorado, the Mexican American median was 10.1 years, whereas Fresno in California could manage only 6.1 years, with some other relatively prosperous California cities—notably Stockton, Bakersfield, and San Bernardino-Riverside-Ontario not far ahead. The size of the urban area does not always guarantee adequate education. Houston, for example, managed only 6.4 years. There are yet other oddities. In Laredo, a largely Mexican American city, Mexican Americans showed very little gain in years of education between 1950 and 1960, but in the Southwest as a whole, including Texas, they gained nearly two years. Nor did Mexican Americans in San Jose, California gain much during the decade despite important gains in California as a whole. Both Leo Grebler and Thomas Carter suggest that migration of the "better educated" may account for some of the extreme differentials.[16]

More careful study of the available statistics points to some disquieting departures from the Southwest norms at both very young ages and at adolescence. Typically Spanish-surname schooling begins later than schooling for other groups, as shown by a lag in enrollment among the 5- and 6-year olds. Enrollment gaps widen increasingly with every successive age group older than 13. By ages 20–21 only 12.1 percent of the Mexican young people are going to school compared with 21.2 percent of all persons in the Southwest. Teenage enrollment lags not only behind Anglo enrollment but behind nonwhite enrollment in all five states. Rural areas are markedly less successful in keeping Mexican youngsters in school than are urban areas.

Signs of progress appear when nativity categories are analyzed. No other factor so clearly accounts for educational differences as does the gap between generations. However, after the foreign-born (median 4.4 years of education for men) and the great increase of the first United States-

16 Grebler, *The Schooling Gap*, p. 19; Thomas P. Carter, an untitled study on Mexican American education, to be published by the College Entrance Examination Board. Carter's research was sponsored by the Mexican American Study Project under a grant from the CEEB.

TABLE 4-3

MEDIAN YEARS OF SCHOOL COMPLETED BY PERSONS
OF 25 YEARS AND OVER, BY ETHNIC GROUP,
IN 35 METROPOLITAN AREAS, 1950 AND 1960 [a]

Standard Metropolitan Statistical Area	1950 Total Population	1950 Spanish-Surname	1960 Total Population	1960 Anglo	1960 Spanish-Surname	1960 Non-white	Schooling Gap 1960 (%) [b] Spanish-Surname	Schooling Gap 1960 (%) [b] Non-white
Abilene	10.1	n.a.	11.7	12.0	4.0	8.8	67	27
Albuquerque	11.7	7.7	12.2	12.5	8.7	10.9	30	13
Amarillo	11.3	4.7	12.1	12.2	8.1	9.5	34	22
Austin	10.9	3.5	11.7	12.3	4.4	8.6	64	30
Bakersfield	9.9	6.5	10.8	11.4	7.3	8.5	36	25
Beaumont-Port Arthur	9.7	7.0	10.8	11.7	8.7	7.1	26	40
Brownsville-Harlington-San Benito	6.3	2.7	7.9	12.3	3.9	9.5	68	23
Colorado Springs	11.7	8.4	12.3	12.4	10.1	12.1	19	2
Corpus Christi	9.4	3.2	10.1	12.2	4.5	8.0	63	34
Dallas	11.0	4.4	11.8	12.1	6.4	8.6	47	29
Denver	12.0	8.0	12.2	12.3	8.8	11.4	28	7
El Paso	9.2	5.2	11.1	12.4	6.6	11.7	47	6
Fort Worth	10.7	5.4	11.4	11.9	7.7	8.7	35	27
Fresno	9.8	5.6	10.4	10.7	6.1	8.8	43	18
Galveston	9.4	4.9	10.3	11.3	6.9	8.3	39	27
Houston	10.4	5.2	11.4	12.1	6.4	8.8	47	27
Laredo	5.4	5.2	6.7	n.a.	5.4	n.a.	n.a.	n.a.
Los Angeles-Long Beach	12.0	8.2	12.1	12.3	8.9	11.1	28	10
Lubbock	11.0	1.7	11.6	12.1	3.1	8.3	74	31
Midland	12.1	1.8	12.4	12.6	3.7	8.8	71	30
Odessa	10.4	3.9	11.4	11.8	4.6	8.8	61	25
Phoenix	10.6	5.3	11.6	12.1	6.1	8.5	50	30
Pueblo	9.1	6.3	10.2	11.0	8.1	9.2	26	16
Sacramento	11.3	7.9	12.2	12.3	9.1	10.9	26	11
San Angelo	10.2	2.9	10.7	11.5	4.0	8.0	65	30
San Antonio	9.1	4.5	10.0	12.1	5.7	9.4	53	22
San Bernardino-Riverside-Ontario	10.9	6.7	11.8	12.1	8.0	9.8	34	19
San Diego	12.0	8.1	12.1	12.2	8.9	10.7	27	12
San Francisco-Oakland	12.0	8.9	12.1	12.3	9.7	10.2	21	17
San Jose	11.4	8.0	12.2	12.4	8.3	12.0	33	3
Santa Barbara	11.8	7.0	12.2	12.4	8.3	9.9	33	20
Stockton	9.1	7.2	10.0	10.7	7.5	8.2	30	23
Tucson	11.2	6.5	12.1	12.3	8.0	7.8	35	37
Waco	9.4	2.9	10.3	11.0	5.5	8.2	50	25
Wichita Falls	10.3 [c]	4.5 [c]	11.4	11.7	6.3	8.7	46	26

born generation (median 8.4 years of education for men) the next generation shows no important improvement. It seems likely therefore that progress in the future will be much harder. However, the older and badly educated immigrants from Mexico will become an even smaller proportion of the population.

In 1960 an extremely small proportion of Mexican Americans reached college. Only 5.6 percent of persons aged 14 or over could report "some college"; four times as many Anglos reported some college and twice as many nonwhites attended college.[17] Nor do Mexican Americans enter the more prestigious colleges. No single branch of the University of California had as many as 100 Mexican students, according to an informal survey taken in 1967, even though persons of Mexican ancestry made up 11.8 percent of the population of the state in 1960.[18] Contrary to conventional ideas about the role of women in Mexican culture, the average schooling of Mexican-American young women is about the same as for men, that is, women do not drop out of school more than men do. Notably fewer women reach the college level, however.

Some hope for future progress can be based on the current increased federal aid to education, especially because the notable advances between 1950 and 1960 were achieved without such help. On the negative side, there is some evidence that some of the federal aid to southwestern schools may tend to reinforce current practices of segregation, as will be discussed in Chapter Five.

[17] Grebler, *The Schooling Gap*, p. 13.
[18] Active recruitment policies undertaken in 1968 altered this slightly.

Notes to Table 4-3

Source: U.S. Census of Population, 1950, PE no. 3c Tables 8 & 9; Vol. 2, Parts 3, 5, 6, 31, 43, Table 42; County & City Data Book, Table 2, Item 28 and Table 3, Item 28.

U.S. Census of Population, 1960, PC(2) 1B, Table 13; Vol. 1, Parts 4, 6, 7, 33 and 45, Tables 73, 77 and 103. Census tracts, Table P–1, P–4, P–5. Reprinted in Leo Grebler, *The Schooling Gap: Signs of Progress* (Los Angeles: University of California, Mexican American Study Project, 1967), p. 18.

a No data for the Spanish-surname group are available for 2 of the 37 metropolitan areas in the Southwest, which are omitted, and no nonwhite data are available for one of the areas shown in the table.

b Computed as follows: the difference in median school years completed between Anglos and, respectively, Spanish surname and nonwhites is calculated as a percentage of the Anglo school years completed. Thus, for example, a difference of three years is equivalent to 33% if the Anglo median is 9 years but to 25% if the Anglo median is 12 years.

c Data for Wichita Falls were incomplete in 1950; Archer County unavailable for Spanish-surname persons.

In a general way, throughout the Southwest, wherever the educational gap is large for one minority it is large for another. Thus a community in which Mexican youngsters are badly educated is also one in which Negroes or (in New Mexico and Arizona) Indians are also badly educated.

The educational disparities shown in Table 4–3 probably reflect primarily then the degree of isolation imposed by a community and confirmed by the schools of the community. This degree of general social isolation may very well be the unknown variable in median educational attainment. There is evidence (Chapter Five) that the degree of segregation in a community is indeed reflected inside its schools. No broad-ranging studies of residential segregation and its association with school achievement exist for Mexican Americans in the Southwest, although, in a general way, it seems that highly segregated cities.tend to educate their children less effectively. Because the residential patterns of some of these cities (Dallas, Fort Worth, Waco, Denver, Houston, Los Angeles, Lubbock, Phoenix, San Antonio, Austin, San Angelo, Tucson) result in a more rigorous separation of Mexican Americans from Negroes than from Anglos, such a study will have to be done cautiously.[19] In general, the variations from state to state can be at least partly explained in terms of the historical position of the Mexican Americans in combination with the general effort made by the individual states to educate all their children. Thus California's 1964 expenditure per pupil in average daily attendance in public elementary and secondary schools was $565. In Texas the comparable expenditure for the same year was $396. These differences are broadly consistent with minority educational attainment in each of the states.

Again it is important to keep in mind the often substantial variations in the quality of education. Even inside a single urban school system such as that of Los Angeles, some predominantly Mexican schools provide inferior education. City to city variations inside a single state as, say, Laredo to Tyler to Houston in Texas, may be of great importance for Mexican Americans.

[19] For an index of the exact amount of residential segregation in large southwestern cities see Joan W. Moore and Frank G. Mittelbach, *Residential Segregation in the Urban Southwest: A Comparative Study*, Advance Report 4, especially Table 2 (Los Angeles: University of California, Mexican American Study Project, 1966) p. 16.

Using a measure that ranges from zero to 100 in increasing degrees of segregation of two populations from each other, we found that the mean segregation index for Mexican Americans from Anglos fell at 54.5; that for Negroes and Anglos at 80.1, and that for Mexican Americans and Negroes at 57.3. There was considerable variation from city to city, ranging in the case of Mexican American segregation from Anglos from a low of 30 in Sacramento, California to a high of 76 in Odessa, Texas.

THE IMPACT OF POVERTY

By any yardstick, especially measuring housing, health, and community services, Mexican American poverty is oppressive. In some respects American citizens of Mexican descent are poorer than any other sizable minority in modern America, though this fact has been largely unnoticed.

Measured in terms of family incomes that fall below a federally defined poverty level of $3,000, a very large 35 percent of all such families in the Southwest were Mexican American in 1960.[20] A larger percentage were classified as nonwhite. But when income is considered in terms of the number of individuals in a family depending on that income, Mexican American families can be shown to fall nearly at the bottom of the ladder. In California, the most prosperous of the southwestern states, the median *income per person* in a family was only $1,380, whereas nonwhites earned $1,437 and Anglos, $2,108 per person. Mexicans are overrepresented among the poor, and especially among the poor children, of whom 29 percent in the Southwest were Mexican American. By contrast only 22 percent of the poor children were Negro and slightly less than half were Anglo.[21]

The available statistics further understate the impact of poverty among Mexicans by ignoring individuals not in families. There are many of these. Typically, the poor family is slightly smaller than other families, including a disproportionate number of single individuals (many aged persons) and broken families. Thus Spanish-surname persons, regardless of family status, constitute 23 percent of the total poor in the Southwest. These 1960 figures are even more impressive when set against the general background of comparative affluence for the nation and for the Southwest.

For example, bad housing is one consequence of poverty. In urban areas of the Southwest more than one-third (34.6 percent) of the Mexican families lived in overcrowded housing in 1960.[22] Less than 8 percent of the comparable Anglo families must inhabit such housing and only 22 percent of the nonwhites. Mexicans are more crowded than nonwhites in all five states—almost twice as crowded as Negroes in Texas, for example. Arizona's Mexican population is nearly as badly off, with 43.6 percent of

[20] Much of this section is based on Mittelbach and Marshall, *The Burden of Poverty.*

[21] Mittelbach and Marshall, *The Burden of Poverty*, p. 5.

[22] The standard definition of overcrowded housing is 1.01 persons per room. If the standard were lowered to 1.5 persons per room, the proportion of Mexican families falling below this standard would not change importantly. Mittelbach and Marshall, *The Burden of Poverty*, p. 43.

the state's 25,391 Mexican families in overcrowded homes in sharp contrast to Arizona's wide-open spaces, cheap land, and recently built cities.

The quality of housing for Mexican Americans is also poor. The incidence of dilapidation in 1960 is seven times as great among housing units occupied by Mexican Americans as among homes occupied by Anglos. "Dilapidation" is an important standard: for instance, nearly always it is associated with inadequate plumbing facilities. However, as Frank Mittelbach points out, there has been considerable improvement since 1950, although the improvement simply narrowed a very substantial gap. In terms of dilapidated housing the Mexicans were worse off than nonwhites in California, Texas, and Colorado. Only in Arizona and New Mexico, with their large populations of badly housed Indians, are the Mexicans slightly better off than nonwhites.[23] Apparently a slightly larger income per family than for comparable nonwhites is almost always more than offset by the large size of the Mexican American families: nowhere is this effect reflected more acutely than in housing.

Beyond the bald statistics of dilapidation and overcrowding, the general impression of Mexican American living areas in the Southwest is seldom very pleasant, though the green yards of parts of East Los Angeles reflect the better economic circumstances of the Los Angeles minority as faithfully as do the miles of dusty, unsanitary shacks in San Antonio. In general, the sudden disappearance of ordinary urban facilities when a visitor enters exclusively Mexican poverty areas is striking. Streets are unpaved; there are no curbs and sidewalks or street lights; traffic hazards go unremedied, and the general air of decay and neglect is unmistakable. (In many cities in the Southwest, "improvements" considered normal and essential in other neighborhoods are financed by per capita assessments of local property owners. These special assessments are often impossible to obtain in poor neighborhoods.) Abandoned automobiles, uncollected refuse, hulks of burned out buildings and the famous cactus fences symbolize the civic status of these neighborhoods. In addition, it is typical of Mexican American neighborhoods in the Southwest that they are carelessly zoned. Thus cheap shops, small factories, small tumble-down houses and even tiny urban farms sprawl together in unregulated confusion. Some Mexican communities are historically the older parts of new cities (Los Angeles, Tucson, San Antonio), and others are nothing more than the decaying remnants of company towns and labor camps. (See Chapter Two.) For the most part these areas did not enjoy the great rise in land values so characteristic of the urban Southwest. Thus too often there is neither new housing, replacement housing, nor much more than mini-

23 Mittelbach and Marshall, *The Burden of Poverty,* p. 45.

mum maintenance. In many *barrios* the only buildings that seem to be in good repair throughout miles of residential blocks are those sheltering the churches, clinics, schools, and welfare agencies so typical of any American slum area.

Inevitably illness and earlier death are the companions of the overcrowded, undernourished poor. The poor tend to consult physicians late in illness and in many communities they lack confidence in the physician and professional health worker.[24] Unfortunately, state and local health agencies generally list their clients as simply "white" or "nonwhite," so the evidence on sickness and mortality among Mexican Americans is very incomplete. We do know, however, that in 1960 Colorado Mexicans were much more likely than Anglos to die from accidents, influenza, and pneumonia. Mexican American infants were three times as likely as Anglo babies to die at birth.[25] Certain other causes of death (chronic heart disease, malignant neoplasms, and vascular lesions) are much less frequent among Mexicans than among Anglos. There is also a marked difference in longevity: the Mexican Americans living in Colorado die more than 10 years earlier than Anglos (if they live more than one year after birth). Deaths from rheumatic heart disease, pneumonia, and automobile accidents are particularly frequent. There are so many fatal motor vehicle accidents among youthful Mexicans (43 percent of all deaths in the age group 16 to 25) that they have become a matter of concern.[26]

In San Antonio, another city for which there is some health evidence, the death rate is also higher for Mexicans than for Anglos in any given age group except the very old. Here also high infant mortality is the rule, although recent efforts have brought infant deaths down considerably. Again there were few deaths from heart disease, cancer, or vascular lesions in 1964. The pneumonia rate is higher among Mexicans in San Antonio than among Anglos. Pneumonia is a typical disease of poverty, and the relative absence of deaths from heart disease, cancer, or vascular lesions probably reflects the unusual age distribution of the Mexican American population. It is to be expected there would be fewer such deaths in an extremely young population.

But acute illness is only one consequence of poverty. There are other

[24] A. Taher Moustafa and Gertrud Weiss, *Health Status and Practices of Mexican Americans,* Advance Report 11 (Los Angeles: University of California, Mexican American Study Project, 1968).

[25] Moustafa and Weiss, *Health Status and Practices of Mexican Americans,* p. 5. Neonatal deaths, defined as "death at birth" with or without prematurity, reached 13.6 percent of the total deaths. The rate for the Anglo population was only 4.3 percent.

[26] Older automobiles, poorer equipment, and lack of adequate training among Mexican Americans are believed to cause this disproportion. Moustafa and Weiss, *Health Status and Practices of Mexican Americans,* p. 7.

varieties of illness that handicap wage-earners and impoverish families without being "acute." A California survey taken in 1954 and 1955 showed, surprisingly, that Mexican Americans reported suffering from less chronic disease than either Negroes or Anglos. Moreover, the incidence of reported chronic disease declined with income (although no physical examinations were conducted in this survey). Figures on specific diseases are occasionally available from local health departments. In the case of tuberculosis, to follow one survey, it appears that in 1963 and 1964 the rate of tuberculosis among Mexicans in Nueces County (Corpus Christi), Texas, was four and five times that of Anglos.[27] A federal manpower project (Operation SER) that is now training disadvantaged Mexican American workers in 23 separate projects in four southwestern states reports physical disabilities (particularly uncorrected defects of vision) as a major cause of trainee dropouts. Moreover, a SER project in Goodyear, Arizona concerned with retraining of Mexican American agricultural workers reported in 1969 that back ailments (from "stoop labor") were so widespread in workers over 50 years of age that they could normally be expected in half the trainees in this age bracket.

In the case of mental illness, a recent set of studies allow no definite conclusions and almost no clues concerning the possible dominance of either cultural or socioeconomic factors. Nonetheless Moustafa and Weiss suggest that mental illness seems to affect younger Mexican Americans more than it does older ones. Mental retardation is certainly higher among Mexican Americans than among Anglo population, although the over-representation is entirely among those with I.Q. scores of over 50. These "higher level" mental retardates are those most likely to be retarded because of cultural and familial factors rather than genetic factors and, most important, to be reported retarded because of problems in test instruments.[28] There is no evidence that there is any "racial" explanation for these rate differentials: Mexican Americans are too heterogeneous genetically for any such explanation to be plausible for any health pattern. Nor is there much evidence that in the aggregate Mexican American health practices significantly affect their general health, though a large and interesting literature on folk medical beliefs and practices would appear to suggest the contrary. In some very poor and some isolated communities and among older people folk remedies appear to be used, but where modern facilities are made available in the large cities, there appears to be comparatively little reluctance to use them.[29]

[27] Moustafa and Weiss, *Health Status and Practices of Mexican Americans*, p. 26.

[28] Based on analysis of residents of Pacific State Hospital in California and on an unpublished community survey conducted in Riverside, California by Jane R. Mercer.

[29] Most information about the persistence of Mexican folk medicine is based on research into enclaves deliberately selected for their low acculturation. In general, use

Poverty may also breed crime, both youthful offenses and adult crime, although very little is known specifically about Mexican American crime. Whatever the hypotheses about crime, culture, and poverty, Mexicans share disproportionately in arrests and convictions in two types of offenses. One is youth crime, particularly activities related to the often vicious gangs in large urban areas. The other is narcotics offenses.[30] Some writers link both of these patterns to traits of Mexican culture. Beyond this assumption that these two types of offenses are an outgrowth of Mexican culture, (which is sharply challenged by Mexican Americans familiar with the situation) we know so little about how Mexicans fit into the structure of organized crime in such cities as Los Angeles, San Antonio, and Phoenix that it is hardly possible to comment on crime as a possible, if deviant, avenue of economic mobility. Then again, much of the reported crime rate is affected by visibility of the Mexican American population and by techniques of police surveillance and judicial practices. It is conventional and probably reasonable to suspect that poverty breeds crime in one way or another, but the specifics of the causal process among Mexican Americans are still unknown.

---

of the neighborhood *señoras, curanderas,* and *parteras* is declining rapidly to almost nothing in the urban centers holding most of the Mexican population. Here again information is fragmentary, but Maricopa County in Arizona reports that 90 percent of their Mexican American babies are born in hospitals. Nueces County in Texas reported 95 percent hospital babies in 1962. The percentage of Mexicans holding health insurance was, for example, very close to the Anglo rate in California in 1955. With rising income, the rates become even closer. Moustafa and Weiss, *Health Status and Practices of Mexican Americans,* Chap. 5.

30 See Joseph Eaton and Kenneth Polk, *Measuring Delinquency* (Pittsburgh: University of Pittsburgh Press, 1961) for a comparison of Mexican American, Anglo, and Negro delinquency rates in Los Angeles. Mexican and Negro rates are higher than Anglo rates, as would be expected; Mexican American patterns are unusual only in the low rates of female delinquency. The authors suggest that this pattern is a reflection of the family structure, in which girls are protected. See also Celia S. Heller, *Mexican American Youth: Forgotten Youth at the Crossroads* (New York: Random House, Inc., 1966), Chap. 5. Mexican American youth are heavily involved in narcotics offenses, although, as social workers in the field point out, increased evidence points to the underreporting of narcotics activities among college youth and its overreporting among Mexican American youth. As one official put it in an interview, "For years in Southern California the narcotics problems was defined as a Mexican problem." Though this image is changing, it is still important in law enforcement activities. Narcotics traffic is significant throughout the border region, not only because marijuana is raised in Mexico, but because Mexico is in entrepôt for narcotics transported from Asia. The degree of participation of Mexican Americans in this traffic, however, is unknown.

The first confrontation of Mexican Americans with American society involved a relationship between two separate societies, each with its own institutions. But Mexican institutions did not long survive the arrival of Anglo American settlers. Thus Mexicans coming to the Southwest in the twentieth century passed into Anglo society as a minority confronting Anglo institutions. The "little Mexican church" of the 1930s and the "little Mexican school" were never, in fact, Mexican. They were an integral part of the American Catholic church (probably with a Spanish, Irish, or French priest) and of a segregated American school system.

Unlike many new ethnic groups, the Mexicans did not bring or invent their own institutions to ameliorate life in the *barrios*. There were some self-help and burial insurance societies, but these societies never reached any real significance. No priests came from Mexico with the immigrating Mexicans. Only in a very few isolated places were there any Mexican-administered Spanish-language schools. Perhaps even more important, the Mexicans did not enter an area where government was committed to even a small degree to welfare state measures, as did the Puerto Ricans or the Negroes moving into the northern cities from the American South.[1]

American Institutions in the Mexican Experience

This chapter will discuss the work of the institutions most concerned with Mexican Americans. First and most important of these is the public school system.

THE SCHOOLS AND THE CHILDREN

There is no doubt whatever about the massive failure of southwestern schools to educate Mexican American children. The magnitude of this failure is detailed in Chapter Four in the bare statistics of dropouts, low achievement, and low grade attainment of Mexican Americans throughout all the Border States. The schools themselves perceived this reality only since the 1930s. Before that time there could have been no

[1] Oscar Handlin, *The Newcomers* (Garden City, N.Y.: Doubleday & Company, Inc., 1962).

recognition of success or failure because there was no problem defined as such—and hence no special effort to educate Mexicans. Nearly all educators saw the Mexican as an outsider to our society, not to be expected to participate in American life. As Carter states,

> Frequently attitudes were tinged with racial prejudice; the literature emphasized the differences between the two cultures rather than their similarities. The typically low intelligence test scores were used as "evidence" of innate inferiority. This in turn was used to justify the commonplace segregation in the schools. Although some concern was expressed for the state of the Mexican-American's health, most of the literature reveals little interest in his economic or educational plight.[2]

Once the problem was recognized and defined as a "problem," then there were attempts to cope with it by explanation. In the process many shallow and overgeneralized stereotypes regarding Mexican children and Mexican culture attained institutional validation as "reasons" for the disproportionate failure rates. It is plain that many Mexican children are bilingual. Educators often saw *the* explanation of Mexican school problems in this bilingualism, assuming that it is detrimental to intellect and thus to the child's "teachability." A second generalization was that Mexican American culture produces "lack of motivation." Cultural traits conceptualized on this shallow level were used to explain the behavior of Mexican Americans in places as diverse as Laredo, Los Angeles, and the villages of northern New Mexico. It was applied to new immigrants from the vast landless peasantry of Mexico as well as to second generation residents of the large cities of the American West. A study of a Los Angeles high school in 1938 from the University of Southern California produced this very typical conclusion, a minor masterpiece of Lysenkian genetics, as quoted by Thomas Carter:

> The Mexicans, as a group, lack ambition. The peon of Mexico has spent so many generations in a condition of servitude that a lazy acceptance of his lot has become a racial characteristic.[3]

This evaluation of the effect of language and culture has become somewhat more sophisticated in recent years, although it is still widely held that Mexican American children are the products of a folk culture dominated by traditional values that make it difficult for them to learn in American schools. Many educators believe that most Mexican Amer-

[2] Thomas P. Carter, untitled study sponsored by the Mexican American Study Project under a grant from the College Entrance Examination Board (Los Angeles: University of California). A revised version of the study will be published by the CEEB.

[3] Lillian Graeber, "A Study of Attendance at Thomas Jefferson High School, Los Angeles, California" (Master's thesis, University of Southern California, 1938), p. 97, cited in Carter, untitled study (1967), p. 64.

ican children are essentially "alingual" (or "bicultural illiterates"), not truly speaking either Spanish or English.[4] The culture is also blamed for the self-derogation that is held to be characteristic of a larger than normal percentage of Mexican children, especially adolescents. Mexicans have been further supposed to be characterized by an apathetic, non-competitive attitude.

This emphasis upon language and culture in the schools of the Southwest is becoming an important theme for many educators of Mexican American ancestry. For them, the idea of maintenance of culture and language has become the cornerstone in a developing ideology attempting to provide solutions for the obvious educational problems of Mexican American children. Though such ideas have been voiced by Mexican American intellectuals in the past,[5] they are now being incorporated into the attempts of new associations (such as the Association of Mexican-American Educators) to influence policy.

Once cultural differences and language difficulties were recognized, certain important steps were taken by southwestern schools to deal with the "unassimilable" Mexicans. In the past the physically segregated school was a natural reflection of the prevailing belief in Mexican racial inferiority. No southwestern state upheld legally the segregation of Mexican American children, yet the practice was widespread. Separate schools were built and maintained, in theory, simply because of residential segregation or to benefit the Mexican child. He had a "language handicap" and needed to be "Americanized" before mixing with Anglo children. His presence in an integrated school would hinder the progress of white American children. As Thomas Carter summarizes the arguments:

> Also mentioned, especially in the earlier literature, were such "facts" as Mexican-Americans are dirty, disease-ridden, and have low moral standards. Separation was seen to be to the Mexican-American's benefit, so that they could better overcome those deficiencies. Additionally, separate schools provided a form of protection; Mexican-American children would not suffer from having to complete with Anglos and thus would not feel inferior.[6]

Segregation practice, however, often belies the theory. "Mexican schools" generally had vastly inferior physical plants, poorly qualified

---

[4] Even the word "alingual" is a pedantic distortion of the obvious ability of Mexican American children to communicate with their parents and peers in some language.

[5] See, for example, Marcos de Leon, "Wanted: A New Educational Philosophy for the Mexican American," *California Journal of Secondary Education,* 34 (November, 1959); George I. Sanchez, "History, Culture, and Education," in *La Raza: Forgotten Americans,* ed. Julian Samora (Elkhart, Ind.: University of Notre Dame Press, 1967).

[6] Carter, untitled study, p. 74.

teachers, and larger classes. Negro children were sometimes assigned to these schools (implying their low social status), and there was a notable lack of effort to enforce the weak school attendance laws. At secondary level schools, students were often simply discouraged from attending school at all. A 1944 study in Texas showed clearly that segregation became more rigid at higher grades, although the "language problem" should have been solved by the later years of school. Further, separate classification was made in some instances on the basis of a child's Spanish name rather than by any test of English language competence. These practices were not ended until a series of court cases in 1946 and 1948 showed both the intent and the practice of segregation.

Segregation is now illegal, but separation remains one of the principal institutional patterns. *De facto* segregation based upon patterns of residential segregation is still widespread in the Southwest. These community patterns appear in single schools and in school districts. This was true in California (although not as drastically as for Negroes) as late as October of 1966, even in the smaller districts.[7] This survey showed that 57 percent of Spanish-surname children in the eight large districts (with 50,000 or more children) attended "minority schools." In a sample of the smaller districts in California, 30 percent of the Mexican American children were found to be attending minority schools—thus the segregation was less severe in these smaller districts. Spanish-surname teachers were also segregated: in the larger districts 51 percent were employed in minority schools.

Some educators still defend separate instruction for Mexican American children on the grounds that it benefits the children. It is supposed to lessen competition with Anglo children and allow Mexican students more time to make up language deficiencies and other handicaps. In Texas there is much stronger feeling then elsewhere among educators against mixing Mexican American children with majority group children. Generally "community opinion" is the principal rationale. These patterns appear to be changing, however. In general it is safe to say that desegregation is under way, but very slowly, and the rate of desegregation still varies widely from one community to another.[8]

[7] California State Department of Education, *Racial and Ethnic Survey of California's Public Schools, Part One: Distribution of Pupils, Fall, 1966* (Sacramento: California State Department of Education, 1967).

[8] The national trend toward minority control of community schools, notable among Negroes in major eastern metropolitan areas in 1968, may well reverse the trend toward desegregation of Mexican schools. The irony of the situation can be illustrated by a case in Riverside, California. A predominantly minority school was recently desegregated only after strong opposition from Mexican American parents had been overcome. The parents liked "their own" school, despite high dropout rates in the junior high school.

Besides *de jure* and *de facto* segregation, there is evidence to suggest a system of separate grading. In the Los Angeles school system, lower-status pupils seem to be quite unconsciously graded and promoted differently in the lower-status schools.[9] The criteria applied in lower-status schools produce a form of "social promotion." Thus lower-status schools move the student (and his unresolved problems) up to the next level, by giving passing grades regardless of performance. As a result, an increasing discrepancy appears between grade-level performance and performance on standardized tests. By the ninth grade many California Mexican pupils have reached the legal age for leaving school and proceed to drop out. Furthermore, "social promotion" permits non-dropouts to drift marginally through high school and then, after high school, to be firmly excluded from higher education. This social promotion happens less to Anglo students in the middle-status schools. In upper-status schools it scarcely happens at all. Grading on non-achievement related criteria obscures a discrepancy between real learning and what is supposed to be learned, and the school can pretend to be an efficient agency. Tensions between the school and the community (a growing factor in Los Angeles) can be kept at a minimum. Only the individual suffers.

Mexican children are also sometimes separated by a special curriculum. Various forms of ability grouping or "tracking" are widely and increasingly practiced in the Southwest. Socioeconomic class and track placement are related: with few exceptions, children from poor homes score below norms on school achievement. Thus Mexican American children are substantially overrepresented in the lower tracks in southwestern schools. Secondary school tracking is well established, and elementary school tracking is becoming more common. By junior high school nearly all children are tracked, and by high school it is very nearly impossible for a student to change his track. Most educators approve of tracking, but many regard the test instruments used to determine track placement with some suspicion, not only because of the usual middle class biases but also because test instruments have not been standardized on Mexican Americans.

An extreme form of tracking is the "special education" class for children classified as mentally retarded. Thomas Carter's study again shows a heavy overrepresentation of Mexican children among the "mentally retarded." California schools in 1966 reported that 27 percent of the

[9] See C. Wayne Gordon, David Nasatir, Audrey J. Schwartz, Gordon E. Stanton, and Robert Wenkert, "Educational Achievement and Aspirations of Mexican-American Youth in a Metropolitan Context," unpublished study, UCLA Mexican American Study Project, undertaken in cooperation with the Board of Education of the City of Los Angeles. A condensed version is presented in Leo Grebler, et al., *The Mexican American People* (New York: The Free Press, 1970).

children in special education classes were Mexican Americans,[10] though Mexican Americans constitute only 13 percent of the total student population. All other available evidence from studies now in progress (see Chapter Four) indicates that this overrepresentation is a gross and insensitive reaction to Mexican language and culture. There is at this date no acceptable evidence of genetic inferiority of any racial or national groups.

Carter concludes that probably very little of this reaction to Mexican language and culture is deliberate, although the effect is just as damaging as if it were. A second reaction, quite deliberate, can also serve to isolate Mexican children. Federal financial assistance has encouraged southwestern educators to develop "compensatory education" programs to help Mexican American children compensate for certain inadequacies they display when compared to a "standard" middle-class child. The idea of "cultural disadvantage" provides a rationale for action to overcome the minority group child's real or assumed deficiencies. It is designed not to change the school but to change the child.

In Texas and California these programs are remedial and concentrated most heavily in language arts and reading instruction. Also important among the programs were "English as a second language," pre-first grade (Headstart) instruction, and other types of remedial instruction. It is very nearly impossible to evaluate their educational effectiveness and as yet, no generally accepted approach to overcoming "language deficiency" exists. All the projects surveyed, however, are concerned with changing "problem" behavior, rather than changing schools, particularly *barrio* schools, to accommodate the child.

Another major technique for dealing with the language and culture of the "ethnic deviant" has been simple suppression. The inevitable result, of course, is a great emphasis upon conformity to the means of instruction. Outright prohibition of the speaking of Spanish in the classroom is probably the most extreme example. The pedagogical arguments for prohibiting Spanish are 1) English is the national language and must be learned; 2) bilingualism is mentally confusing; 3) southwestern Spanish is a substandard dialect; and 4) teachers don't understand Spanish. Absolute prohibition of Spanish still exists in many southwestern schools, often enforced by corporal punishment.

Other cultural differences are often severely suppressed as well—the poorer and more "Mexican" the school, the more severe the suppression. Dress codes are rigidly enforced; hair is forcibly cut; first names are often changed. (The name "Jesús" in particular seems to disturb teachers and is nearly always changed to "Jesse.") Carter concludes that "the lower

[10] California State Department of Education *Racial and Ethnic Survey*, pp. 36–46, cited in Carter, untitled study, p. 109.

the social class level of the student body, the more rigidly the child is expected to conform to the educator's image of the perfect middle-class teenager." Secondary schools observed in Texas seemed particularly restrictive about dress and behavior. California schools, on the other hand, were the least restrictive.

Yet another technique for handling cultural deviation lies in the teaching of a prescribed curriculum. Every school is given some latitude in the content, method, and sequence of the material taught; but lower-status schools are more likely to adhere rigidly to state or local curriculum guides without special regard for discrepancies between the curriculum and the home background of the children being taught. As a rule, such unmodified adherence tends to favor middle-class Anglo-American children, not the children from other ethnic groups. Similar rigidity is found in techniques that emphasize rote learning of certain elements of the content that teachers feel are "fundamental and distilled." The traditional school year, September to June, often forces the children of migrant farm workers out of school for many weeks.

Only spasmodically has a flexible approach been taken to adapt schools to diverse local situations. In large part there is even failure to realize that schools, particularly those serving heavily Mexican areas, can be modified in many ways. In most states changes are largely confined to equipment purchases, hiring better staff members (psychologists, for example), or some special curricula. By institutional standards the compensatory education programs mentioned above are already a success. They require little institutional modification, tend to placate spokesmen for the ethnic population, strengthen the role of school administrators, and create new functions inside the educational establishment. In some areas efforts are made to relate schools to their client communities by hiring Mexican nonprofessionals, although this practice is still rare. Other programs not strictly remedial are in effect, although only a very few schools have entertained or practiced the notion that they might be radically changed in order to serve their community more adequately. Even in the critical area of teacher re-education only the barest beginnings have been suggested. California funded only one program in 1965–1966 designed to develop more efficient methods of teaching Mexican American children.

Teachers in the Southwest actually have very little material available on the teaching of Mexican Americans. Professional schools tend to use general treatises on "cultural disadvantage," very few of which emphasize Mexican Americans. One of these, from Science Research Associates (1966) describes Mexican family roles in the most traditional terms.[11] Another recent manual (1962) by Miles V. Zintz repeats all the ancient stereotypes.[12] Mexican Americans are alleged to (1) devalue formal education, especially for women; (2) consider success in terms of nonmaterial rewards; (3) be present-time oriented; (4) be conservative and not desire change; (5) be patient, conformist, and perhaps apathetic; (6) become imbued with a *mañana* attitude and (7) be nonscientific.

Recent studies of teacher attitudes suggest that these guides conveniently support and amplify conventional (and quite unsuccessful) approaches to Mexican American children. Perhaps more important, such guides justify school failure by placing the blame for nonadaptation on the Mexican family. Teachers in the Southwest quite generally ascribe institutional problems to the failure of the Mexican family to prepare the child for school,[13] overlooking the problem of ignorance among educators. This author saw recently a manuscript prepared for the National Education Association that began a guide to the learning capacities of the Mexican child with a discussion of Aztec culture. Although Aztec culture interests Mexican children, it is irrelevant when teachers must deal with urban children in a modern urban context. This (and other irrelevancies) tend to deflect teacher interest and to "build a wall" around real children with real problems.

Whatever the lag between knowledge and the implementation of knowledge inside an institution, any general views of education in the American Southwest should be supplemented by some information about the variations between cities. We know very well the great difference in other institutions, such as the relative lack of social welfare services in San Antonio.

One recent study of Los Angeles suggests that an urban area with substantial resources can do much better than other systems.[14] Here the metropolitan system is so large that centralized administration, common programs, and uniform financial support and personnel policies produce a great deal of uniformity between the "Mexican" schools and the "Anglo" schools. Still, the southwestern pattern continues in Los Angeles. More than one-third of the Mexican American children enrolled in Los Angeles secondary schools drop out before completion. In some schools, slightly more than half are able to finish. Mexican American pupils gen-

---

11 Kenneth R. Johnson, *Teaching the Culturally Disadvantaged Pupils*, Unit Four (Chicago: Science Research Associates, Inc., 1966), page 5; cited in Carter, untitled study, p. 41.

12 Miles V. Zintz, *Education Across Cultures* (Dubuque, Ia: William C. Brown Co., 1963), cited in Carter, untitled study, p. 44.

13 Carter, untitled study, pp. 34–70.

14 Gordon, et al., "Educational Achievement," p. 4.

erally score lower than others in four dimensions of achievement: academic grades, deportment, achievement test scores standardized against a national norm, and I.Q. test scores. On achievement tests and I.Q. tests Anglo students scored slightly above the national norms and Mexican Americans, well below.

Contrary to information in the guides used by the teachers, this study found that most Mexican American students want formal education after high school.[15] Most even *expect* some education after high school. Occupational aspirations are also high. More than half of the Mexican teenagers want skilled or professional white collar positions. In attitudes, the noticeable differences between Anglo students and Mexican American students gradually narrow as they progress through school. So pronounced is this narrowing of differences that by twelfth grade (that is, among those students who have survived the public school system) there is very little difference between the two groups in values and expectations.

This same study tried hard to isolate the factors in the background of the students that might affect Mexican American performance in the Los Angeles system. The study found that the most consistent and important influence is the educational level of the family; the economic level was less important. Moreover, the exclusive use of English in the home contributes to good performance in school. Certain pupil attitudes and values are also important. In addition, the general school context (that is, the ethnic composition and social class level of the school) seems to be exceedingly important.

It appears that some awareness of the critical importance of the school system has begun to affect the Mexican community itself. In Los Angeles this new awareness appeared vividly in March, 1968 when four heavily Mexican American high schools were boycotted by a group of Mexican American students. The community-based organization that appeared as a result (Educational Issues Coordinating Committee) has served a significant function for the city of Los Angeles ever since the boycott, and has even been incorporated in the system as a formal advisory body.

CATHOLICS AND MEXICANS

As institutions, churches can serve to socialize values in childhood and to maintain a form of social control over values and conduct in later life. Most Mexican Americans consider themselves Roman Catholics. No even reasonably close guess of the exact number of Mexican Catholics is

---

[15] Gordon, et al., "Educational Achievement," p. 38.

available but it is probably no less than 95 percent of the total population of Mexican Americans in this country.

Generally it is true that the Mexican identification with Catholicism acted to strengthen the already acute isolation of Mexicans from the predominantly Protestant Southwest (Chapter Three). But to assume that the Catholic church in the Southwest was a strong institution from the first days and strong enough to affect importantly the lives of the first great waves of Mexican immigrants is misleading. A recent study of the historical record of the archdioceses of Los Angeles and San Antonio back to the time of the first American settlement shows that, whatever its desires or intention, the church could do little to protect or help acculturate Mexicans.[16]

When the United States acquired the Southwest and its new "charter member" minority, the Catholic church in the region was very near collapse. The magnificent mission properties had been expropriated by the Spanish and Mexican governments and acquired by large Mexican and Anglo landowners. The residual fragments of the missions that were concerned with strictly religious activities became ordinary parochial churches, quite isolated one from the other in a vast territory, lacking either clergy or the means of supporting a clergy. The new American bishops were not much more than "padres on horseback."

They received some help from the priests of various religious orders, most of them from foreign countries. These included the Oblate Fathers from France, who appeared in 1847, Spanish Franciscans (once charged with service of the mission system), Spanish Claretians, Immaculate Heart Mission Fathers, Vincentian Fathers and Piarist Fathers. These men and a few native priests administered only the most essential religious services over a vast area. The burden was staggering for this small group of overworked and overextended clergy. We can pick a single year in the late nineteenth century (1890, in the archdiocese of Tucson) and find a lone parish priest trying to bring the basic sacraments of baptism, marriage, and burial to 1,052 Catholics spread over an average area of 7,000 square miles. In 1890 in the combined dioceses of San Antonio, Corpus Christi (including Brownsville), El Paso, Santa Fe, Tucson, and Los Angeles (including Monterey and San Diego) there were only 193 parish priests, and of this tiny number only 14 had Spanish surnames. (French, Irish, and even Spanish priests worked with the Mexicans. Mexican Americans have

16 Patrick Hayes McNamara, "Bishops, Priests and Prophecy: A Study in the Sociology of Religious Protest," (Ph.D. dissertation, University of California at Los Angeles, 1968), condensed in Grebler, et al., *The Mexican American People.* This study explores the history of the church generally in the Southwest, as well as in San Antonio and Los Angeles, and also utilizes survey data on Catholic practice from the two latter cities.

never been and are not now likely to become Catholic priests. The reasons for this lack of interest are unknown.)

It appears, in fact, that in these early years the bishops could at best hope for survival. The later mass immigrations from Mexico brought the Catholic church hundreds of thousands of nominal Catholics. The new immigrants were probably as unused to American Catholicism (with its heavy and rather ascetic Irish influence) as was the average Protestant. Moreover, many immigrants, fresh from the revolutionary church-baiting of Mexico, were anticlerical. The immigrants appear, indeed, to have come from precisely that population group in Mexico among whom Catholic influence was weakest. They were unaccustomed to parochial schools, financial support of the church, religious instruction, and regular attendance at Mass, all of which are important to American Catholics. Even the basic doctrines of Catholicism were so mixed with remnants of rural Indian paganism that the church, in summary, saw the new Mexican immigrants as likely "new converts" but not as true practicing Catholics. As McNamara says,

> Contrary to the notion that the immigrant would seek out the Church for support and comfort, the Church had to reach out for the newcomer if it was to perform its function. This would have been difficult under the best of circumstances. The poor resources at the command of the Southwestern church made it an overwhelming task.[17]

Only very slowly was it possible for the church to move away from narrowly pastoral goals in the Southwest. In part, this advance was helped by substantial gifts from Catholic sources in the Midwest and East. The church began to interest itself more substantially in the building of parochial schools and in Americanization of the Mexican population. Both of these motives were inspired, to a large extent, by the desire to defend Mexican Americans against Protestant missionaries and to keep Mexican youth from entering a public school system that was at least latently anti-Catholic and publicly devoted to strictly secular values. However, the available resources were never enough. Even the effort put forth by the Archdiocese of Los Angeles (the richest of the southwestern religious divisions) was extremely limited. Settlement houses appeared in Los Angeles in 1905, and a Bureau of Catholic Charities appeared in 1919 (there was none in San Antonio until 1941). Even a massive drive for a total system of parochial schools achieved only very limited success. By 1930 the combined archdiocese of San Diego and Los Angeles had 301,775 Catholics but only 79 schools. By comparison, Baltimore (with approximately the same number of Catholics) had 179 parochial schools in 1930. El Paso

[17] McNamara, in Grebler, et al., *The Mexican American People.*

and Corpus Christi lagged then even more: El Paso had 12 schools for a Catholic population of 119,623 and Corpus Christi, 27 schools for 247,-760 Catholics. Nearly all the Catholics in these Texas cities were Mexican Americans.

All of these extensions beyond pastoral goals were characterized by a certain defensiveness in the public statements and publications of the hierarchy. This was particularly apparent in Los Angeles after the "zoot suit" riots of the early 1940s. Moreover, there had been no protests from the church during the Mexican repatriations of 1930 through 1933. When the Mexicans became a visible social problem during the Los Angeles riots, the church wanted to show Anglo citizens that the church was an institution determined to instill American ideals into the laity. These objectives included such diverse efforts in the Mexican community as citizenship instruction, classes in English, and youth activities of the type exemplified by the Catholic Youth Organization. Very often these socialization efforts were combined with anticommunist instruction.

After World War II the Los Angeles hierarchy began a massive program of parochial school construction in the Mexican areas of the city. Its completion by 1960 was, significantly, hailed by Catholic leaders as an important step in safeguarding the Catholic faith of Mexican Americans and (with a trace of the old defensiveness) in demonstrating that the church was an institution that was determined to instill American ideals into the laity.[18] It may have been equally true that this very expensive system of parochial schools served not only to defend the faith but to maintain the cultural and social distinctiveness of Mexicans, although no special effort to this end appears to have been made. In any case the hierarchy could keep Mexican American children away from the assimilative influence of the public schools and simultaneously claim credit for efficient Americanization. McNamara sees the parochial system and the new but very limited sallies into social welfare as basically designed to defend the faith and not, except accidentally, to promote assimilation.

Social action designed to promote a more abstract goal than defense of Roman Catholicism appears in San Antonio as early as 1943 but then under the pressure of great poverty. In the words of Archbishop Lucey:

> A very general lack of labor organizations, the absence of good legislation and the greed of powerful employers have combined to create in Texas dreadful and widespread misery. The evil men who are driving tens of thousands of our people into a slow starvation will be held to strict accountability by the God of eternal justice.[19]

18 McNamara, in Grebler, et al., *The Mexican American People.*
19 McNamara, in Grebler, et al., *The Mexican American People;* citing *The Spanish-speaking of the Southwest and West* (Washington, D.C.: National Catholic Welfare Conference, 1943), pp. 3–4.

Archbishop Lucey's eloquence did not stir any action until 1945 when, characteristically, practical help came not from the resources of the local church but from the American Board of Catholic Missions in Chicago, which set up a "Bishop's Committee for the Spanish-Speaking." Mc-Namara points out that the typical southwestern Catholic parish churches, locked into association with the dispossessed Mexicans and very poor, have been exceedingly vulnerable to economic pressure, particularly from Anglo Catholics. Thus when direct social action has appeared, it nearly always has been instigated by a group well outside the area of local pressure.

There are yet other reasons for lack of interest in social welfare among parish priests. Some San Antonio parish priests, interviewed only recently, felt their people were not yet ready for the social teachings of recent Popes; others simply lacked interest or training in the social doc-trines of the Roman Catholic church.[20] Yet the need for social ameliora-tion in San Antonio is so obvious that when the opportunity for obtain-ing federal money appeared in 1964 through the Office of Economic Opportunity, San Antonio church projects became the single most impor-tant device for funneling these funds into poverty areas in that city.

Quite generally, the Roman Catholic Church, whatever its inten-tions, has been quite unable to mediate between Mexicans and the Anglos in the larger society. Like the educators of the Southwest, the church has also suffered from misperceptions. Except perhaps in San Antonio, the ruling spirits of the Roman Catholic church have been reluctant to take the ideological lead in any of the important issues of past or present for Mexican Americans. Certainly they greatly overestimated the appeal to Mexicans of Communist organizers and underestimated the steady move of Mexican Americans to large urban areas. They viewed assimilation into American life as desirable, but their unwillingness to push assimila-tion unless Catholicism were also maintained makes it unlikely that they could ever have been a very effective force. Perhaps more important, the bishops sensed that any pushing of social issues was likely to embitter the larger Anglo Protestant population. Whatever the views of the church hierarchy from one decade to another, the church never was able to involve Mexican Americans in the institution itself. (The bishops of the late nineteenth century greatly feared inroads by a very small group of Protestant missionaries. It appears now that the Protestants never real-ized their opportunity.) The measure of this lack of involvement is that priests born in Spain still are highly desirable for service in the arch-diocese of Los Angeles, because they speak the language.

---

[20] McNamara, in Grebler, et al., *The Mexican American People.*

MEXICANS AND LAW ENFORCEMENT

Law enforcement agencies may have been as important as the public school system in forming the attitudes of Mexicans toward the United States—certainly they have contributed to a prevailing "culture of suspicion." [21]

There have been good reasons for this distrust and resentment: a combination of certain characteristics of the Mexican American community and the reaction of law enforcement agencies to those characteristics. First of all, Mexicans are visible, and most Anglos in the Southwest have thought of them as foreigners. In all cities and towns Mexicans traditionally are associated with the impoverished, crime-prone sections that directly concern local peace officers. In addition, Mexican Americans have had prolonged and unpleasant contact with one federal law enforcement agency in particular—the Border Patrol of the U.S. Immigration and Naturalization Service. Only Chinese immigrants share this experience with the immigration agency.

Southwestern law enforcement agencies have always been concerned with Mexicans. The Texas Rangers were founded in 1835 specifically to cope with the "Mexican problem" of the Texas Republic and they survive to this day as a token force. As an elite law-enforcement agency, the duties of the Texas Rangers still occasionally require control of Mexican Americans. Further, the Western tradition of vigilante law enforcement (and the chronic shortage of salaried peace officers) meant that in the nineteenth and early twentieth centuries the employers of Mexican labor could deputize men to serve their private interests. Arizona mine owners, Texas ranchers, and California fruit growers did this frequently in labor disputes with their Mexican laborers.

Important today is the peace officers' sphere of control. The more local the jurisdiction of a deputy or patrolman, the more he can exercise personal discretion. Thus the small-town policeman reflects the local social structure and its degree of benevolence or repressiveness. On the other hand, the Texas Rangers were controlled by the state of Texas rather than by individual Texas towns. This meant only a *potential* restraint over their behavior. The importance of this potential became manifest (after many years) when a Mexican-American state legislator in Texas was able to force an investigation of their treatment of Mexicans. The results of

21 For a study of San Diego indicating that this is the case, see Joseph D. Lohman, et al., *The Police and the Community*, U.S. President's Commission on Law Enforcement and Administration of Justice, Field Survey No. 4 (Berkeley, Calif.: 1966), p. 55, also Lawrence Glick, "The Right to Equal Opportunity," in Samora, ed., *La Raza.*

this investigation led to the reduction of the Texas Rangers to a token force. More recently, in the 1960s, some arbitrary actions of the Rangers against Mexican Americans during the melon strike in Rio Grande City got the Rangers into trouble. Once again, the standards of the entire state rather than a local area were invoked.

In this sense, the most controlled of all these groups is the Border Patrol because, unlike local law enforcement officers, it must enforce federal law over a vast area. Thus, although southwestern history is filled with violence and illegal acts by local officers, the much more controlled efficiency and wide-ranging authority of the Border Patrol has made it greatly feared. Border Patrol officers are highly trained. Over the years they have been built into a disciplined force with remarkable *esprit de corps*. They must not only stop entry of illegal aliens but enforce all pertinent federal laws affecting the heavy traffic in people and goods across the border between the United States and Mexico. Thus a single Immigration Service patrol officer (representing the laws and regulations of some 25 federal agencies) can, for instance, stop a car carrying members of a Mexican family anywhere on a California highway. The officer's wide authority allows him not only to question the right of every member of this family to be present in the United States but, in addition, to enforce a wide range of federal laws. Thus *la Migra* (the Border Patrol), whether operating in Chicago or Denver, Los Angeles or Fresno, may appear to the ordinary Mexican immigrant as the rude, inquisitive, dangerously arbitrary power of a hostile government. Moreover, local officers can always put considerable pressure on visible Mexicans by merely threatening to summon the Patrol. A California highway patrolman reported his contact as follows:

> 4–28 male, age 27. Packing house worker (Mexican national) cited for weaving in roadway. Subject was apprehensive but aware of violation. Negative toward questions, asserted ignorance, unable to understand or speak English. Subject was then asked to show passport, but still showed negative compliance. He was then informed that the Border Patrol would be contacted for assistance. Subject became more open, a little English spoken. He then presented a California drivers license.[22]

The magnitude of this threat to Mexican Americans cannot be overestimated. Even the interviews and paperwork of a friendly agency (employment, social security, public school, health agency) may at any time involve a Mexican immigrant family in a hopeless tangle of trouble.

Few other kinds of American citizens are called upon in their own country to produce proof of citizenship. For Mexican American citizens

[22] Henry T. Levesque, "Ethnic Groups and the Police Officer" (unpublished manuscript).

these checks are greatly resented. Decades of raids (sometimes in the night to avoid missing the head of the family), mass deportations (3.8 million removals from 1950 to 1955 during Operation Wetback), and the casual violence that sometimes erupts during the interrogation of a group of brown faces have left pervasive fear in the community. Today a government car with federal license plates can still drive into a Mexican neighborhood and be preceded by warning cries from the small boys: "La Migra!" Today in the normal pursuit of its duties the Border Patrol still swoops down on garment factories in East Los Angeles and packing sheds in Sacramento: the hired help is lined up for a routine citizenship check. At present these raids and interrogations are concentrated in areas that employ large numbers of unskilled Mexican workers and in important transportation centers. For example, Riverside, California, was the outermost limit to which a "blue card" holder could visit in the United States. Riverside therefore became a center of both Border Patrol activity and illegal labor contracting. Every Greyhound bus heading north is stopped and checked fifty miles from the border.

It is true that the traffic in illegal aliens is widespread, lucrative, and accompanied by an increasingly sophisticated trade in false documents. It is also true that among law enforcement agencies, the Border Patrol is notably scrupulous about staying within its mandate to enforce certain federal laws. It is also well trained, well disciplined, and quite aware that the enforcement of laws against narcotics smuggling and illegal labor contracting is often very dangerous. Nonetheless the reputation of the Border Patrol for efficient ferocity still lingers among Mexican Americans.

That its reputation should be so negative, even today, is in a way paradoxical, because in terms of socioeconomic gains, the modern Mexican American owes much to the efficiency of the Border Patrol. Illegal aliens in Texas and in the large cities of the Southwest always supplied a reservoir of cheap labor to undercut the most minimal gains of "legal" Mexicans in farm labor or in other badly paid occupations. Illegal aliens were used to help break strikes: as recently as 1967 it appears that Texas melon growers used aliens to break an agricultural strike. (Thus, in the lower Rio Grande valley, Mexican American organizers found themselves running a patrol boat on the Rio Grande as unofficial and unpaid assistants of the Border Patrol.) In past years there was good reason to suspect that active lobbying by American industrial and farm interests helped keep the Border Patrol understaffed and underpaid.[23] The relationship between low wages and a steady supply of illegal aliens is perfectly clear to Mexican American union people and to many community leaders.

[23] Ernesto Galarza, *Merchants of Labor: The Mexican Bracero Story* (San Jose, Calif.: The Rosicrucian Press, Ltd., 1965), p. 61.

Yet the immigration experience is so recent for many Mexican Americans and the memory of poverty in the old country so vivid that much natural sympathy for the "wetback" still exists. This feeling was demonstrated tragically in Los Angeles in 1968 when a young man from Hermosillo hid himself inside the undercarriage of a jet aircraft, hoping to be carried to the United States. When the aircraft lowered its landing gear the body of the man, frozen to death, fell into the city of Los Angeles. Newspaper inquiries led to a destitute and desperate family—and to a great deal of community sympathy. In time, as the proportion of native-born Mexican Americans increases, it is highly probable that the immigration experience will fade and possibly with it some of the bitterness about the Border Patrol—at least, outside the border area.

Mexican Americans also have a special history and a special relationship to certain federal conservation agencies. To the villagers of northern New Mexico and southern Colorado the modern conservationist approach to public lands (enforced by certain federal agencies) is a serious source of conflict. The conflict occurs at many points, of which lost or modified grazing rights may be the most important. The withdrawal of certain public lands from public grazing of sheep and cattle seriously damaged the economic life of some villages. Recently militant Mexicans in New Mexico struck back in a variety of ways: confrontations, sit-ins, and deliberately set forest fires were only a few of the reactions to conservation policy. That national forestlands and watershed areas should be closed to livestock (except for a system of very restricted grazing permits) and open to vacationing tourists only adds insult to injury. In this relationship Mexicans are not thinking of a national interest in erosion or recreational areas. The remembered wrong, fresh and important, is that the ancestral lands of the Mexican and the Indian were taken away without the consent of the "owners" and that use of them is now restricted.

Behind much of the bitterness of Mexicans toward law enforcement agencies is the tendency of southwestern law enforcement agencies to define Mexican Americans as prone to crime. Mexicans in most cities live in areas that are traditionally poor. The Mexican "quick smile and quick knife" is a folklore stereotype in the Southwest that has led to a sort of amateur anthropology—even in the highest levels of the police administration of the largest city in the Southwest. In 1960 Chief William H. Parker of the Los Angeles Police Department gave his official view:

> The Latin population that came in here in great strength were here before us, and presented a great problem because I worked over on the East Side when men had to work in pairs—but that has evolved into assimilation—and it's because of some of these people being not too far removed from the wild tribes of the district of the inner mountains of

Mexico. I don't think you can throw the genes out of the question when you discuss behavior patterns of people.[24]

All poor classes of people are generally exposed to police scrutiny as potentially "dangerous." For the Mexican Americans there is a special twist—they may also be "illegal." Furthermore, they are associated in the public mind with narcotics. As we noted earlier, until very recently the traffic in narcotics throughout the Southwest was defined almost entirely as a Mexican problem.

Any of the past studies of the relationship between Mexican Americans and peace officers reflects violent contact with the police. Beginning with the investigation by Paul Taylor in 1931, we find reports of habitual police violence and disregard of civil rights in the Rio Grande valley in Texas, in Dallas, Denver, and in Los Angeles.[25] All of these urban police departments except in the Rio Grande valley were in their time modern, relatively *controlled* law enforcement agencies. In truth, police incidents attract attention only when the violence reaches some unusual degree.

Even in 1967, two deaths in two nights in Riverside County in California failed to be noticed in the newspapers of nearby Los Angeles, perhaps reflecting community indifference to Mexicans. In this incident, one teenager choked to death while vomiting in a Corona police lockup. The next night in nearby Riverside his companion was shot to death by a police officer while "resisting arrest." A coroner's jury noted that the bullet entered the boy's back below the beltline and left the body in the front of the skull. Many Mexicans concluded the boy had been helpless when shot. The verdict of justifiable homicide enraged the community and brought out pickets, but the issue soon died down everywhere except in the Mexican American community. Neither the two deaths nor the subsequent reaction in the community interested nearby Los Angeles. Police brutality and the habitual violation of civil rights have been facts of life in the Mexican American communities of the Southwest.

All available evidence indicates that Mexican relations with the police in these cities are very dissimilar from those of Anglos. A study of the 1938 Los Angeles Superior Court records showed that the ratio of arrests to felony convictions was 5.3 for Mexican Americans compared with only 2.7 for Anglos. Probation was awarded almost three times more frequently to Anglos than to Mexican American offenders. The authors

24 *Hearings before the United States Commission on Civil Rights* (San Francisco, Calif., January 27, 1960 (Washington, D.C.: Government Printing Office, 1960).

25 Paul S. Taylor, "Crime and the Foreign Born: The Problem of the Mexican," *National Commission on Law Observance and Enforcement, Report on Crime and the Foreign Born* (Washington, D.C.: Government Printing Office, 1931) and *National Commission on Law Observance and Enforcement, Lawlessness in Law Enforcement* (Washington, D.C.: Government Printing Office, 1931).

of the study report that "prejudicial treatment" and arrest procedures and the use of "indiscriminate, wholesale 'dragnet' methods" helped account for the higher arrest-conviction ratio.[26] Thus Mexican American relations with the police in the cities are similar to those of Negroes. A staff report for the U.S. Commission on Civil Rights states:

> In general, the Spanish-speaking population echoes the complaints of the Negroes. These people feel that they are the objects of unequal law enforcement and that insufficient effort is expended by governmental organizations (including the police) to communicate with their groups.[27]

Committees to deal with law enforcement agencies are a standard feature of almost any Mexican American community action group. Unfortunately, these very limited and very recent efforts to guarantee minimum civil rights are now masked by the much more vocal and aggressive Negro militancy.

OTHER INSTITUTIONS

Mexican experience with other official institutions is very much like the experience of any other immigrant group—with exceptions that are generally quite easily accounted for by circumstance or historical events.

Three important circumstances in particular affected Mexicans: the border was always very close; Mexican immigrants came in large numbers relatively recently; and the Southwest was peculiarly lacking in either political or ameliorative institutions. The historical events include most notably the use of social welfare agencies to channel Mexicans back to Mexico during the Great Depression.[28] This lesson in practical cooperation between welfare agencies and the power structure of local communities was not lost on Mexicans. On the other side, the very success of these "repatriations" reinforced two important Anglo stereotypes about Mexicans. Mexicans are "foreign"; Mexicans are "passive."

Officials in public agencies almost always comment on the passive "hard-to-reach" character of the Mexican approach to public agencies. The exact word varies but the problem is the same: Mexicans are not responsive; they withdraw; they are uninterested; they lack aggressiveness. Various cultural explanations are advanced (sometimes by Mexican

---

[26] Edwin M. Lemert and Judy Rosberg, "The Administration of Justice to Minority Groups in Los Angeles County," *University of California Publications in Culture and Society*, II, eds. R. L. Beals, Leonard Bloom, and Franklin Fearing (Berkeley and Los Angeles: University of California Press, 1948), 3, 12.

[27] Staff Paper, "Spanish-Speaking Peoples," submitted to the United States Commission on Civil Rights (February 5, 1964), p. 47.

[28] See Chapter Three for a discussion of the repatriation programs.

leaders); but it is at least as logical that Mexican Americans are simply distrustful and suspicious. Ultimately the activities of almost any public agency depends upon the coercive power of the state, and Mexicans are sensitive to this power.

Several recent studies of health agencies conclude that Mexican Americans often avoid using them because of cultural conflicts in the definitions of health, causes of disease, and means of treating disease. From these studies have come some important training programs for reaching the Mexican community. But most of the studies also note, sometimes almost in passing, that the public health worker is greeted in the Mexican American home just as is any other government worker, as somebody coming to cause trouble.

However, the effects of historical accidents fade in time. There are now fewer foreign-born Mexicans. More Mexican American professionals enter public service and can at least "speak the language" of bureaucracy. Mexicans who move into Anglo areas benefit by a better image in the eyes of law enforcement agencies. There is some new and growing Mexican American political redress power, particularly in the larger cities. Federal experiments in antipoverty programs, moreover, had given new perspectives to public agencies and to clientele communities.

It is possible that the many new programs may have succeeded in shifting the meaning of government to the poor, but it is too soon to know. Some recent programs have helped Mexican Americans, some are nothing much more than token, and some others may have done harm. Whatever their effect in ameliorating poverty, at least one important side effect in Los Angeles (and possibly in other cities) has been a period of friction with blacks. Generally the OEO grants have tended to reward groups and communities that are fairly well organized. The black community in most southwestern cities has a distinct edge over the Mexican community not only in internal organization but in well-established lines of communication to Anglo institutions. Thus in Los Angeles the black community seems always to have gotten a disproportionate share of grants and projects. This disparity has become an incentive to Mexican American organizations.

In general it has been the tendency of the Office of Economic Opportunity to fit new programs into a network of existing agencies. As might be expected, this has tended to slow down or stifle entirely any movement for social change that might occur outside of existing institutions. For Mexican Americans it may very well be that the greatest accomplishment of OEO has been that of focusing attention on Mexican problems and the sources of their discontent. This tendency is well illustrated in the case of the single largest federal project to relieve Mexican unemployment,

Operation SER. Funded in 1966 by OEO as "Plans for Progress, Inc.," this group used the existing organizational structure of the League of United Latin American Citizens and the American G.I. Forum (See Chapter Eight) to create a giant antipoverty project. Operation SER now guides 23 separate community projects in five states (Arizona, California, Colorado, New Mexico, Texas). There is no doubt that the primary purpose of the project to find jobs and training "slots" for the chronically unemployed, has been quite successful. The projects use existing lines of leadership, compete with Negro groups in every city for entry-level jobs in training programs and private industry, and in general, are most successful when they approach private and public groups as an instrument of tokenism.

Existing agencies (public school systems, employment services, and so forth) used by SER are often so resistant to change that, in effect, SER must either establish duplicate facilities for Mexicans or in some measure counsel its trainees in the techniques of avoiding discriminatory practices of the very agencies that are supposed, by contract, to cooperate with them. Neither the OEO nor the Department of Labor has done much to fight the limitations of existing local bureaucracies. This single largest Mexican American manpower development project is at this writing so much a prisoner of its time and the existing network of bureaucracy that it is very hard to regard it as any kind of departure from traditional relationships between the Mexican American and the instruments of government.

In recent years it has become plain that the fate of America's distinctive subgroups depended upon the reaction of American institutions—much more so than upon any institutions the group may have generated within itself. Whatever the sentimental attractions of a completely separate community, such a community never has actually worked. Even the vigorously self-sufficient notions of most black separatists depend ultimately upon a complex structure of institutions. In New York City, to name a center of such sentiment, even a single group of schools cannot operate without a complexity of institutions. The separation of the Ocean Hill-Brownsville school district needed, just to begin, the cooperation of the state of New York and the cooperation of a powerful teachers' union. Separatism may even require the very sophisticated willingness of certain American institutions to allow experimentation upon their institutional bodies. But the romantic ideal of the separate community persists perhaps only because it *is* romantic, and simple. Thus, following Oscar Handlin we suggest that the degree of Mexican American assimilation or adaptation depends upon the reaction of American institutions.

There is another facet to interaction between the ethnic community and the institutions. Something in the subculture may inhibit or facilitate the use of institutions by specific groups. Jewish and Japanese children, for example, march off to school with enthusiasm: Mexican and Negro children are much less interested. Some sort of cultural factor works here. In this chapter, without considering any degree of "native" enthusiasm, we have described only the institutional end of the interaction. Thus Mexicans were at first defined by the schools of the Southwest as "outsiders" and "foreign." A forcible approach to Americanization simply did not work as it had worked earlier with other immigrant groups. Perhaps this was simply because earlier groups were residents of large cities whereas Mexican immigrants tended to remain in isolated rural villages or work camps. Gradually the old perception gave way to a new one, that the "problem" concerned cultural differences encompassing the Spanish language and Mexican culture. It appears now that the new definition limits the school systems, once again, in ways of changing themselves. In poorer schools in isolated areas the new perception may be no more than a mask for prejudice. In the schools of wealthier Los Angeles, problems of language and culture appear to be a rationale for a double standard of achievement.

The interaction between the Roman Catholic church and the Mexican was more positive, but there is no evidence that it was natural or easy. Certainly Mexican needs were seen from the beginning as at least an obligation, and all of the resources of a very poor institution were bent to this end. In later years an exclusively pastoral concern gave way to a view of Mexicans as needing Americanization. Still later, Mexican American Catholics are beginning to be seen as an American minority subject to much overt discrimination. Perhaps the church will use this definition in some areas as the background for a new appeal for social justice. Recent militant actions as, for example, taken in Los Angeles by *Catolicos por la Raza,* may accelerate the process of making the church more responsive.

The schools and the church have a mandate to change "their people," but law enforcement agencies only react to a given quantity. Their strategy, since they always operate with inadequate staff, is to concentrate on areas with known high crime rates and other acute social problems. This strategy has always meant some real risk of discriminatory action. There is little evidence of a change, even in institutional definition, in this regard at the local level, though law enforcement at the state and federal levels has varied widely and changed over time.

Probably one of the most important problems in a transformation of American society is the position of minorities in the society's institutions—their capacity to make use of the institutions individually or collectively. The voluntary associations, like the Catholic Church, have one set of problems; government agencies, like the schools, have a quite different set. Possibly one of the most important features of the government agencies is that for the poor, the institutions dealing with law enforcement may become inextricably linked with the institutions dealing with health, welfare, and education. This may happen totally apart from either the intent or the awareness of the "welfare" agencies. Behind all government-funded agencies is the power of the state: to accomplish their avowed socialization or ameliorative purpose their repressive potential must not only be recognized but neutralized by their officials. Otherwise the charge that these are in fact "white racist" institutions may, in the view of the minority, be all too well founded.

It should be plain by now that Mexican Americans are a complex minority. They live in a wide variety of situations in a region of the United States that is changing with great speed. To be sure, they share with other minorities the problems of poverty and certain strains attendant upon a slow and painful emergence into participation in urban American life. At the same time they reflect some of the original diversity of the Southwest of an earlier age.

For example, many Mexicans still live in the uplands of the upper Rio Grande river, in an isolation and bitterness that have enveloped them for a century. This atmosphere reached a point of tension strong enough in 1965 to produce a minor rebellion led by Reies Tijerina. (See Chapter Eight.) Moreover, many Mexicans still live in the small towns of borderland Texas, although many of the children are drifting away to the cities to earn a living. These traditional patterns also include hand labor by Mexicans who still leave their homes in Texas every spring to join the migrant farm workers in the fields of California and the Middle West.[1]

Family and Community: Stability and Change

Thus it is that when "Mexican family life" or "Mexican community life" is discussed, we must capture and dissect something that is living, changing, and anything but unitary. It is diverse statistically, historically, and regionally. This diversity is not even a simple matter of generational change, as we shall see. In this chapter we take up the familiar forms of social differentiation: generation, social class, and community type. We will examine the varieties of meaning of each and the significance of each in general processes of change, particularly of change in the family. We will see that linear or straight-line

---

[1] See the series of publications from the study conducted by Lyle Shannon and associates of the University of Iowa, the most recent of which is "The Study of Migrants as Members of Social Systems," *Proceedings of the 1968 Annual Spring Meetings of the American Ethnological Society* (in press), comparing patterns of adaptation of Texas Mexicans and southern Negroes to life in Racine, Wisconsin; and the comparable set of studies conducted by Harvey Choldin and Grafton Trout of Mexican Americans settling in rural Michigan. (Harvey M. Choldin and Grafton D. Trout, *Mexican Americans in Transition: Migration and Employment in Michigan Cities* [East Lansing, Michigan: Rural Manpower Center, Agricultural Experiment Station, Michigan State University, July, 1969].) "Dropping out" of the migrant stream in these Midwestern communities is not a new phenomenon, but it is perhaps an increasingly important one.

change (for example, from first to third generation, from rural to urban setting, from lower-class to middle-class status) does not simply pertain to the Mexicans.

GENERATION: A QUESTION OF PLACE

Generation by generation, immigrant families and their descendants gradually acquire the values and enter into social relationships that make them indistinguishable from the larger society. Leaving aside the question of color, Mexican Americans have acculturated over generations much as immigrants have done, although there are some important qualifications and exceptions.

The most important exception is the different rates at which generations change in different parts of the American Southwest. For example, the bigger cities tend to offer a more open milieu than other areas, but there is variation even between these cities. A second generation Mexican American man in Los Angeles is generally far more acculturated than a second-generation person in a Texas city, such as Corpus Christi. As a consequence, generations of Mexican immigrants are difficult to compare from one city to another. The social milieu of some agricultural towns, on the other hand, is so repressive and offers so little opportunity for economic or social movement that change from one generation to another is almost imperceptible.

The second exception is a group of old-family Spanish Americans who live in northern New Mexico and southern Colorado. They follow traditional occupations, speak English with difficulty, if at all, and appear to be more "Mexican" than even some of the new immigrants from Mexico. In this area generations have meant changes and adaptation, but this adaptation was not an adjustment to urban American values: these people adjusted first to a colonial society hard-pressed by hostile Indians, then to an isolated and alienated minority status under the first United States governments, and then to a set of changed economic circumstances that threatened their very livelihood. No great pressure for accommodation to urban American relationships and values has yet appeared among these people.[2]

[2] See Florence Rockwood Kluckhohn and Fred L. Strodtbeck, *Variations in Value Orientations* (Evanston, Illinois and Elmsford, New York: Row, Peterson and Co., 1961), for an account of traditional life in such a village. Note also Kluckhohn's account of the changes she observed in this village culture between her first research trip in the late 1930s and her later visit in the 1950s. Of these changes, she concludes (p. 257):

There can be no turning back by these people, given the fact that they are firmly held within the borders of the United States and are increasingly subjected to dominant Anglo American culture as one by one the small villages like Atrisco

Any understanding of changes by generation must always be qualified by the milieu in which they are taking place. Accordingly, any intra-United States migration among Mexican Americans is of great importance. We will see later in this chapter that such geographical mobility, indeed, is taking place on a large scale. In effect, this mobility leads many of the more energetic and ambitious away from the small towns. As a result, the Anglo outsider would discern little or no change in the small cities and small towns of the Southwest. Although the local structure of these towns may seem unchanged, however, the *total* situation of this American minority may be radically changed. An analogous example is the American Negro. The great exodus of blacks from the South means that small southern towns may be overtly changed very little, but American Negroes on the whole have changed drastically.

Consequently the meaning of generations to Mexican Americans is very much a matter of geographical location. The significance of a boyhood in Kingsville, Texas, or El Paso strikes Mexicans at once. Third generation Mexican Americans from either of those towns are different from those reared in Los Angeles, as well as from each other. Among the Spanish Americans of New Mexico and Colorado, the consciousness of generational differences takes a different form. Here people can distinguish families that entered the Southwest with the *first* wave of Mexican immigration following the Oñate expedition of 1598 and the "late" waves of the seventeenth and eighteenth centuries. These distinctions are recorded,[3] memorized, and passed along from generation to generation. For a New Mexican, a name like Baca, Chávez, Roybal, Griego, Gallegos, Tafoya, or Montoya evokes a particular lineage, even if the family founder was hanged for thievery. On the other hand, to most outsiders such distinctions are obscured by the efforts of these charter-member *manitos* to distinguish themselves from the newer immigrants from Mexico, whom they called *surumatos,* in a clear-cut division by "generation."

Something of the Mexican interest in Mexican first families has been adopted by an Anglo society that in many areas is still short of a hundred years of settlement. It is part of the occasional local obeisance to "our Spanish heritage." Thus Santa Barbara, California (to name one of many such cities) still puts on an elaborate *fiesta* every year, which pays homage

---

decay and the inhabitants of them move off to urban centers . . . Two alternative end results appear possible. One is that of a greater acculturation of the group . . . The other prospect is a fairly thorough-going disorganization . . . At the moment the first of the two prospects seems the more likely.

3 See Fray Angélico Chávez, *Origins of New Mexico Families* (Santa Fe, N.M.: The Historical Society of New Mexico, 1954), for a fascinating compilation of family histories arranged by "wave."

to the original "Spanish" settlers. (This celebration is, incidentally, still news in the society pages of the *Los Angeles Times*.) In general, however, the California descendants of old families intermarried so heavily with either native Americans or with newer Mexican arrivals that it is extremely difficult to find any "pure" descendants.

Another example of this attempt to establish old family lines is provided by the "Canary Islanders" of San Antonio, Texas. Shortly after San Antonio was founded in 1691 one group of settlers from the Canary Islands was given the equivalent of a patent of nobility and declared *hijos dalgo* (aristocrats) by the Spanish Crown.[4] Ever since, the Canary Islanders have distinguished themselves from the "Mexicans" around them, and today they are a significant segment of upper-status "Spanish" in San Antonio. The more general symbolic significance of this pattern of claiming old-line ancestry is indicated by the fact that during a household survey of San Antonio a very dark, very poor man proudly told the interviewer that he, too, was a "Canary Islander." Thus in many smaller cities as well, the actual or *soi-disant* descendants of such "old families" are among the elite, although they are also among the lower classes. But the lineages are so mixed that a pure-blood old-line group can scarcely be said to exist outside New Mexico and Colorado. Here the original population was large enough from the first years for marriage to be kept largely within the original group.

FAMILY AND CLASS IN
THE AGRICULTURAL TOWNS

In the small towns of south Texas, Arizona, central California and other parts of the Southwest, visitors often express shock at the way Mexican Americans live. The standard Anglo apology, is, "Oh, you should see the way they live in old Mexico!" As noted in Chapter One, it is usually assumed that the benchmark for measuring Mexican American progress is Mexico. Anglos do not seem aware of the assumptions behind this comparison nor would it occur to them to compare Negro homes with African huts.

In part, the appearance of the Mexican *barrios* or lower-class neighborhoods often helps along this southwestern double standard. The poor oftentimes live in shacks or adobe structures (depending on the area) that resemble those of old Mexico. Sometimes the yards are bare and sun-

---

[4] Sister Frances Jerome Woods, *Mexican Ethnic Leadership in San Antonio, Texas* (Washington, D.C.: Catholic University of America Press, 1949), p. 12. She gives an interesting historical analysis of the social structure of the Mexican American community of San Antonio.

baked. Sometimes there are a few cacti and sometimes there is a profusion of flowers. The residents of these *barrios* are largely Spanish-speaking or speak a reasonably stable mixture of Spanish and English. The community depends upon a restricted range of jobs. There are typically a few storekeepers, gas station operators, priests, teachers, attorneys, and doctors (many living outside the *barrio*) who mediate between the laboring majority of the Mexican community and the larger Anglo system. Nearly always these towns look as if there had been no important changes since 1910. This date is not picked at random; the town of Roma in the lower Rio Grande valley of Texas, for example, was used as a site for the filming of the movie *Viva Zapata!* Presumably there had been very little change in Roma from the rural Mexico of Zapata's day. Although Roma now boasts an international bridge over the Rio Grande, not far downstream one can see little flat-bottom boats used to ferry people and freight across the river. And when the cities of Laredo and Nuevo Laredo, a bit further upstream, celebrate their annual *charro's* day, horses are still swum across the river (in violation of custom regulations on the importation of animals) just as they swam in the time of General John J. Pershing.

These *barrio* areas of the small agricultural towns are among the poorest ethnic enclaves in the United States, but this is not as important as the fact that they also act to segregate the poorest Mexicans into visible communities: the more energetic move out; middle-class Mexican Americans (the only group that might act in some manner to modify the Anglo image of the *barrio*) move out into a less segregated part of the community as quickly and as permanently as possible. Others leave the town. (Several *barrios* in the Southwest have the name of "Sal Si Puedes" or "Get Out If You Can"—indicating the local opinion of such a traditional neighborhood.) Thus the Anglo stereotypes are perpetuated by the nature of the *barrio* itself.

The face of the *barrio* may remain substantially unchanged, but there is some internal change. There is some acculturation, although it comes very slowly. Some portion of the developing middle class may remain in the city, although such persons tend to move away. However, the most important change cannot be seen at all. This is the movement of the most energetic, most talented, and perhaps even the luckiest *barrio* residents to larger cities in the same area or to large cities in another area.

In this process the most traditional Mexicans tend to be left behind in the poorest areas. Here traditional patterns are functional and instead of being surprised by their persistence, we should realize that if traditional life did not exist it would have to be invented. Faith healers are far cheaper than good medical service; priests cost less than an attorney;

and it is easier for a migrant family who needs a loan to begin a season on the migrant worker stream to get it from a storekeeper than from a bank. However, it must be pointed out that all of these traditional features of Mexican American life that are taken as quaint or picturesque are associated in one way or another not only with Mexican Americans but with any ethnic group that lives in poverty. Formal resources, such as social workers, are scarce. In Texas, for example, social workers are few because the state of Texas allocates a pittance for social welfare programs. Even the immigration *notarios,* a notable feature of the Los Angeles Mexican "downtown," are almost missing in south Texas; most Mexicans in trouble with immigration authorities in south Texas simply cannot afford *notarios.*[5] In general then, there are few formal resources by which people can become acculturated.

It is clear from community studies that the family is the most important facet of life for Mexican Americans in south Texas as well as in other traditionalistic lower-class enclaves. This is not only the immediate family of husband, wife, and children but the extended family of relatives on both sides. It is the main focus of obligations and also a source of emotional and economic support as well as recognition for accomplishment. Family roles within the nuclear family unit are clear cut; the mother is seen ideally as an embodiment of the Holy Mother. Her daughters are expected to follow suit in their purity, their dedication to the welfare of the males in the family, and in the warmth of their relationship to each other. The woman is to be protected by the man, who must face the vicissitudes and hazards of the outside world. His masculinity (*machismo*) is of great importance; he demonstrates this by physical and sexual prowess, the latter even outside his marriage. His relations with the world outside the family are filtered through other close relationships with a group of friends. These are age peers who depend upon each other for work, pleasure, and various kinds of emotional support.

From this pool of friends the family will draw the godparents of its children. Godparentage (*compadrazgo*) in this sort of traditional system is a method of knitting the community together normatively and of formalizing the informal ties of friendship. The same system of godparentage is found in Mediterranean countries as well as in Latin America.

A man and the godfather of his child become *compadres.* (The *compadre* relationship may also be a way of honoring a person superior

5 A *notario* is a lawyer in Mexico; in the United States, many notaries public upgrade their status in the eyes of their Mexican clientele by a simple and misleading translation. The small towns of south Texas figure in two reports on Hidalgo County: William Madsen's more general treatment in *Mexican Americans of South Texas* (New York: Holt, Rinehart and Winston, Inc., 1964), and Arthur Rubel's analysis of one town, *Across the Tracks* (Austin, Texas: University of Texas Press, 1966).

in status: for example, a boss or *patrón*.) This formalization of the bonds of friendship into a pseudo-kinship relationship is a reliable indicator of the importance of kinship ties to the Mexican Americans. They can be so important that they form the prototype of all significant relationships. It is, in fact, more important as a tie between two age peers than it is as a religious belief or as a tie between godparent and godchild. (As a religious act, it symbolizes formally a promise by the godparent that the child will be brought up as a Christian should anything happen to the child's parents.)

Within the family there is a hierarchical allocation of responsibilities from the head of the household down through the males. Women are sheltered; it is felt that their most meaningful relationships should be within the family. Ideally, their social relationships and recreation should consist solely of visits to cousins and other relatives. They are expected to gossip, to cook the traditional dishes (many requiring a vast amount of hand labor), to look after many children of all ages, and to attend to the needs of their men.

In such communities relations with neighbors, however, can be fraught with hostility. The tight interdependence of the family does not encompass the neighbor, who may, in fact, wish you ill. The fear of witches is not unknown in traditional parts of Texas. It is more likely than not that the "witch" afflicting you with physical or emotional problems is a fairly close neighbor who may envy you (*envidia*). Warmth inside the family and hostility to those outside the family are almost elements of survival in a very crowded area. These are people who live in poverty. Things often go wrong; people get sick for no obvious reason. Houses in these communities are close together; there is often much less room than in the ordinary middle-class suburb. Small mischiefs—a man staring at a neighbor's wife, fruit stolen from a tree, dogs digging up the ground; these are the endless irritations that divide neighbors. But it is also true in the Mexican American *barrios* that many members of extended kin groups build homes next to one another, which might even be called "family compounds." They permit a man to surround himself and his family with people who are close and trustworthy.

Many of the same elements are found in Mexican middle-class life, especially in small Texas towns that are isolated from the mainstream of American life. This isolation continues to a remarkable degree. Although the middle-class Mexican in these towns visits the physician rather than the *curandera*, the attorney rather than the priest, and sends his children to a local college or to a state college some distance away, he remains in a basically traditional environment. He interacts little with Anglos—or even with Mexican Americans outside his own kinship and peer group.

A graduate student at the University of California, Los Angeles, recalls that in four years at the University of Texas in the early 1960s his social relationships were almost entirely confined to other Mexicans and occasionally Latin American students—almost never Anglos. Until he left Texas for California, this student lived in an almost totally Spanish-speaking environment, seldom interacting meaningfully with Anglos at any class level.

It is to some extent valid to describe this world as a caste system: [6] Mexicans and Anglos, sometimes living in the same yet different towns, each with a distinct and separate class system, dealing with each other through intermediaries in both ethnic groups, and with only a minimum of "off-the-job" social interaction. In many respects, in fact, the relationship of Mexican and Anglo in the many small agricultural communities of south Texas and other parts of the Southwest are like the relationship classically portrayed by Davis and Gardner between Negro and white in the Mississippi town described in *Deep South*.[7] There is even a rather frightening counterpart to the Klu Klux Klan. For decades the Texas Rangers terrorized the Mexican Americans of the Rio Grande valley,[8] and even today, although they are reduced in numbers, *los rinches* are still used to "handle" Mexicans. The most recent use of the Texas Rangers was, appropriately, during a strike of Mexican melon workers near Rio Grande City.[9]

Thus it is in the Texas counties with the very large ranches that the analogy with southern Negro-white life is most striking. Such a comparison is valid historically because the plantation model was the Texas

[6] The caste-like characteristics of small Mexican American *barrios* in agricultural towns have been explicitly noted by Walter Goldschmidt, in a study of a central California town, *As You Sow* (New York: Harcourt, Brace and World, Inc., 1947), as well as in several unpublished dissertations. Caste-like conditions in Corpus Christi in the 1920s are portrayed by Paul S. Taylor, *An American-Mexican Frontier* (Chapel Hill, N.C.: University of North Carolina Press, 1934).

The very special situation in New Mexico is analyzed by Donovan Senter, in terms reminiscent of the class-caste distinction, in "Acculturation among New Mexican Villagers in Comparison to Adjustment Patterns of other Spanish-Speaking Americans," *Rural Sociology*, X (March, 1945), 31–47.

[7] Allison Davis, Burleigh and Mary Gardner, *Deep South* (Chicago: University of Chicago Press, 1941).

[8] Stories of terrorization are recounted in Rubel, *Across the Tracks*. The Rangers figure prominently in Mexican border *corridos*, or epic ballads.

[9] See Walter Prescott Webb, *The Texas Rangers* (Boston: Houghton Mifflin Co., 1935), for the story of the Rangers and their origins in border warfare. Even this account, which, though careful and objective, is generally something of a glorification of the group, recounts many stories of Ranger callousness and brutality toward Mexicans in the border areas. A state investigation of the Rangers, initiated by a Mexican American legislator, resulted in the reduction of the Rangers to a token force.

ideal. It is not quite valid today because of the position of upper-status Mexicans in some of the towns and because of the peculiar relationship sometimes found between upper-status Mexican Americans and upper-status Mexicans in Mexico. In many south Texas towns, middle-class Mexicans are indeed in much the same position as are middle-class, small-town southern Negroes. They maintain the middle-class style with fervor and with a conviction that it *is* a good life. But the towns of the Rio Grande valley are somewhat special. Here upper-class Mexican Americans sometimes intermarry with Mexican families across the river. Professional men sometimes keep memberships in Mexican country clubs. Thus the caste-like plantation system breaks down; as professionals or the descendants of original settlers, upper-status Mexican Americans can establish solid claims to prestige. Further, in recent years south Texas has begun to send Mexican American legislators to the state legislature, as do many predominantly small town districts in New Mexico. One county in Colorado is known locally as "the Banana Republic," so great is the degree of Mexican political control there. The first Mexican American federal judge, Reynaldo Garza, comes from Raymondsville in south Texas. (Judge Harold Medina of New York is also of Mexican descent, but his appointment in 1947 had no ethnic implications.) Kika de la Garza, one of two Texas-Mexican Congressmen, also comes from south Texas. New Mexico has regularly returned Mexican senators to Washington; the well-known Dennis Chávez, and at present, Joseph Montoya.

Thus it is plain that the analogy between southern Negroes and whites and southwestern Mexicans and whites cannot be sustained. The Mexicans of south Texas are not all quite in the same subordinate position as are the Negroes of Mississippi, although it should be recalled that in the Rio Grande valley of Texas it is the middle class rather than the total group that exerts a measure of political power and control in a few areas.

VARIATIONS ON A THEME: MEXICANS AND SMALL TOWNS

Even among the small traditional communities there are important differences. A few of these are almost entirely Mexican and control is in the hands of the Mexican middle class. A larger number are dominated by an Anglo power structure. The domination in these areas can be paternalistic or it can be suppressive; doubtless it is often a combination of the two. It is surprising to find some of these towns and small cities in the rich agricultural areas of California as well as the poverty pockets of rural Texas, but California's Imperial, Coachella, and San Joaquin valleys have many such towns.[10]

Many of these communities seem to have been completely bypassed by the enormous growth and expansion of California. Here the local elite are the large agricultural growers. Oddly and significantly, many of the growers are relative newcomers to the United States themselves. In Delano, the scene of a protracted and bitter agricultural strike, the growers are largely Slavic and Italian immigrants who are quite new to this kind of entrepreneurship.[11] But whatever their personal status, both the new and old large-scale employers of Mexican agricultural labor feel themselves embattled and threatened by César Chávez' attempts to organize agricultural workers, something which has never been successful in the past. Some employers attempt to play a paternal role and to help their laborers settle and accept some of the public opportunities available in California. But even more of them simply assume the present inferiority of their Mexican help. In this respect the power structure of these small communities (Delano is only one among them) is little changed from the California agricultural community of a generation ago or from today's small south Texas towns.

There are, however, two important changes, both of them in attitude. First, the climate of both the federal and the state governments for unlimited exploitation of Mexican labor is distinctly unfriendly. Second, Mexican labor itself has new leadership (most notably César Chávez), which is thoroughly familiar with some of the techniques of modern communications, with the climate of national opinion, and with methods of making use of potential political allies. These advantages in climate of opinion and in leadership were never before available to groups of Mexican American laboring men. The change is so crucial that it can be felt even in Texas. Thus, although Texas has a right-to-work law, some beginnings have been made in the unionization of Mexican agricultural labor, even in south Texas.

[10] See Goldschmidt, *As You Sow,* for a Central Valley town in California; Margaret Clark, *Health in the Mexican American Culture* (Berkeley and Los Angeles: University of California Press, 1959), for a study of a very poor *barrio* in San Jose, which is within commuting distance of San Francisco. Recently, Theodore W. Parsons, Jr. completed a dissertation study of a small community close to Palo Alto, home of Stanford University, which is strikingly reminiscent of the south Texas towns ("Ethnic Cleavage in a California School," unpublished Ph.D. dissertation, Stanford University, 1965).

[11] John Gregory Dunne, *Delano* (New York: Farrar, Straus & Giroux, Inc., 1967), presents an interesting journalistic account of the strike and the community. Ernesto Galarza, *Merchants of Labor* (San Jose, Calif.: The Rosicrucian Press, Ltd., 1965) presents a longer perspective on agricultural labor in California. Galarza was active in several efforts to form an agricultural workers' union, and his book is written from the point of view of a participant.

Of the smaller communities we know comparatively little. Much of what we "know" (like so much anthropological knowledge) concerns norms and beliefs: we know relatively little about actual day-to-day behavior and even less about the range of possible variation in this behavior. We do not know as simple and as important a thing as the most gross differences in the behavior of children reared in all-Mexican towns and in partly Mexican towns. It seems reasonable to expect there would be important differences in, for example, identity between the two groups. A poor Mexican child in an all-Mexican town would be lower class; in a predominantly Anglo town, he would also be a "Mex." We would also expect significant differences between the two groups in patterns of neighboring, degree of dependence on the kinship structure, and degree of dependence on other Mexican Americans. At this stage it is only possible to make reasonable guesses and to point out the complexities of Mexican American life even in small towns. The phrase "even in small towns" is appropriate because the complexities are even greater in large cities, where most Mexican Americans now live.

MEXICANS IN THE CITIES

We can see, for a beginning, that the degree of residential segregation of Mexican Americans throughout the largest cities of the border states varies far more than it does for Negroes (Chapter Four). This variation in segregation has important social consequences. One of the indicators of assimilation of any immigrant group into American society is its degree of segregation. In general the new immigrants (from southern and eastern Europe) are more segregated than are old stock (from northern Europe).[12] The fact that patterns of Mexican American segregation vary among cities of the Southwest shows clearly that the usual paradigms of American assimilation of ethnic groups do not apply to this population.

[12] See Stanley Lieberson, *Ethnic Patterns in American Cities* (New York: The Free Press, 1963) for an analysis of segregation patterns of various foreign stock populations. Mexican Americans are not included in his analysis, but their segregation in the Southwest is contrasted with Negro-white segregation in the region in Joan W. Moore and Frank G. Mittelbach, *Residential Segregation in the Urban Southwest*, Advance Report 4 (Los Angeles: University of California, Mexican American Study Project, 1966). The study also analyzes Negro-Mexican segregation. See this book, Chapter Four, for a brief summary of its findings.

Though there is no comprehensive ethnographic account of Mexican American life in the large cities of a generation ago, Carey McWilliams describes Mexican Americans in Los Angeles, in *North from Mexico* (Philadelphia: J. B. Lippincott Co., 1949). Ruth Tuck's fine study of San Bernardino, a citrus-growing community some 75 miles east of Los Angeles, was done during the same period. Interestingly, that large California city appears to be remarkably like a small Texas town in regard to Mexican American life. See *Not with the Fist* (New York: Harcourt, Brace & World, Inc., 1946).

That is, segregation does not decline systematically with length of residence in the U.S.

Because of this extreme variation between cities, we can infer that the rate of change of segregation is different among cities for Mexican Americans. For example, Mexican Americans are escaping the *barrios* much more slowly in Odessa, Texas, than in Los Angeles. This rate of change is not itself a steady, even progress toward acculturation or assimilation. As shown in Chapter Four it seems to depend not only upon changes inside the Mexican community but more importantly, upon changes in the larger community. Los Angeles has more people of Mexican descent than any other city in North America except Mexico City or (recently) Guadalajara. Los Angeles has grown enormously since the late 1920s when Mexicans first began to appear in large numbers. In the 40 years from 1928 to 1968, Los Angeles achieved strong economic as well as population growth. A regional trading city became an economic center of national and international importance. Slowly and with many setbacks Mexicans and other newcomers to the city were caught up in its expansion. (The setbacks peculiar to Los Angeles were the Mexican repatriations of the early Depression years and the serious and recurrent clashes with the police highlighted by the "zoot suit" riots of the early 1940s.) But even throughout the years of setback, Mexicans were carried along by the tide. Increasing numbers moved into the middle class and out of the *barrios*. Sometimes the movement was very much like the traditional invasion-succession cycles familiar to students of ethnic ecology in Eastern cities. Some *barrios* expanded at their periphery and filled in the non-Mexican spaces; and thus the new neighborhood became an expanded *barrio* with a scattered residue of non-Mexican residents and institutions. Again, as freeways cut through Mexican American areas in Los Angeles, whole neighborhoods appear to have been transplanted to other locations. More commonly, prosperous Mexican Americans would move miles away from the *barrios* into completely new housing developments as these new tracts began to fill the brushlands of Los Angeles county after World War II. Thus by 1965 almost no elementary school in the vast sprawl of Greater Los Angeles did not have at least some Mexican American children.[13]

Of course, this school distribution did not mean equal-status interaction in all areas of Los Angeles life. Moreover, even if Mexican Americans were dispersed throughout southern California, in 1965 there were still many thousands of Mexican Americans locked into *barrios* as in south

[13] See California State Department of Education, *Racial and Ethnic Survey of California's Public Schools. Part One: Distribution of Pupils*, 1967.

TABLE 6–1

PERCENT OF MEXICAN AMERICAN RESPONDENTS HAVING PREDOMINANTLY
OR ALL ANGLO ASSOCIATES, FRONTIERSMEN AND COLONISTS,
LOS ANGELES, SAN ANTONIO AND ALBUQUERQUE, 1965–1966

| | | City and Residential Area | | | | | |
| | | Los Angeles | | | San Antonio | | Albuquerque | |
	Frontier	Intermediate	Colony	Frontier	Colony	Frontier	Colony
Work associates	70%	47%	39%	41%	22%	55%	11%
Boss	84	81	73	73	29	54	11
Personal friends	29	11	7	12	1	59	23
Children's friends	66	35	12	34	6	20	0
Children's schoolmates	70	35	15	34	8	21	5
Total number (= 100%)	248	221	254	113	424	51	59

Source: Data for Los Angeles and San Antonio are derived from probability samples of Mexican American households drawn by the Mexican American Study Project, University of California at Los Angeles, and for Albuquerque by Operation SER, Santa Monica, California. We are grateful to both organizations for making the data available.

Texas. Consequently, in Los Angeles being "Mexican" can mean many different things.

The Mexican American who lives in a *barrio* is likely to be different from the individual who leaves an area of ethnic concentration to live with native white Americans. The terminology to describe the two kinds of people comes from Alex Simirenko.[14] He uses the word "Frontier" for the predominantly non-ethnic areas and the term "Colony" for the predominantly ethnic areas. Simirenko studied Russian-Americans, and he noted that the Russian Colonists lived in the area immediately around the Russian Orthodox church; here remained most of the traditionalists. Choosing to remain in the Colony does not mean that an ethnic person is not occupationally mobile. Nor does choosing to live in the ethnic Frontier mean that one *is* mobile. Middle-class individuals may live in Colonies and poor people may live in Frontiers, although generally there is a close association, as one would expect, between poverty and the Colony and higher income and the Frontier. If we apply this idea to

[14] He used these terms in a study of second generation Russians in a Midwest city. See *Pilgrims, Colonists and Frontiersmen* (New York and London: The Free Press and Collier-Macmillan Ltd., 1964). Paul Sheldon gives a portrait of Mexican American leaders of Los Angeles in "Community Participation and the Emerging Middle Class," in *La Raza: Forgotten Americans,* ed. Julian Samora (South Bend: University of Notre Dame Press, 1966).

Mexican Americans, we see that the difference between Colonists and Frontiersmen is that the former is *more likely* to use other Mexican Americans as both a membership group and as a reference group. On the other hand, the Frontiersman is *more likely* to use Anglos. The value of the phrase "more likely" varies from city to city. The deciding factor apparently is the openness of the city to ethnic movement, as shown in Table 6–1. Here we list data for Los Angeles, Albuquerque, and San Antonio in approximate order of expected openness. We see that Mexican American adults and children living in Colonies in all three cities are far more likely than Frontiersmen to have predominantly Anglo friends and workmates, but the differences between cities are remarkable. Mexicans in the Colonies of Los Angeles are almost as likely as Mexicans in the Frontier of San Antonio to have Anglo friends and associates. Once again we can see how importantly assimilation depends upon the degree of acceptance in the larger society. General statements about Mexican American life in large cities must be based upon individual cities as a first step in dealing with this very complex pattern.

CLASS AND MOBILITY

The vast majority of Mexican immigrants were extremely poor, and although a large proportion of them remain poor, many have definitely been occupationally mobile, compared to their fathers. More mobility occurred (Chapter Four) where there was opportunity for education and where there were more and better jobs. How, then, has this change affected Mexican Americans in terms of social class?

To be "upper class" in the American Southwest always meant to be "Spanish," even long before American settlers arrived. It is still true today in Mexico and in any South American or Latin American country with a large population of native Indians. (Thus the myth of "pure blood" was not invented in the United States.) Mexicans of mixed Spanish-Indian blood or of pure Indian ancestry have long suffered from discrimination and exploitation in their own country. When the United States acquired the southwestern territories the elite were "Spanish," and the Spanish-surname settlers were almost entirely of *mestizo* (mixed Indian-Spanish) stock. These were both *mestizos* from Mexico and persons who had become *mestizo* by intermarrying with Indians in the United States. The new American settlers accepted the Mexican status system on its own terms, and it matched their own biases. Most notably, they accepted the "Spanish" as Spanish and as pure-blood persons entitled to superior position. Thus before and after American sovereignty, socially mobile individuals felt pressure to cease being "Mexican" and to become "Spanish." The distinction may appear to be absurd (often the color of the "Spanish" person is notably far from white) but historically it has been exceedingly important to Mexican Americans. (A thousand examples are available. To cite just one: purely Mexican restaurants in the Southwest still attempt to legitimize themselves by advertising a "Spanish" cuisine.)

Because Spanish persons were acceptable, social class mobility was possible even when there was strong race prejudice against Mexicans. Once acceptable in a race-conscious society, the "Spanish" individuals did not hesitate to depreciate the claims of *arrivistes,* no matter how fictional their own claim to status. The establishment of such a "Spanish" upper-status group in new southwestern cities that had no firmly established elite group is a remarkable (and almost unnoticed) fiction of modern Mexican American life. In some cities this need for a fictitious "Spanish" mask for the middle class did not last long, yet it still persists in other cities, reflecting the status anxieties of the local Mexican American community and the prejudices of the Anglos. It may be that some combination of increased numbers and occupational security makes it unnecessary to deny Mexican ancestry. It may also be that the changed recent political climate, with the accompanying attempts by some business firms and colleges to recruit Mexicans, makes it better in some cities to be Mexican than Spanish.

It appears that in many parts of the Southwest (where rapid change has outpaced the evolution of a stable social class system with a clearly defined style of life) many Mexican Americans in middle-class occupations view the occupational system rather instrumentally. There seem, in fact, to be two different types of mobility.

The first is mobility as a means of obtaining enough money to establish higher material levels for the enjoyment of a manner of life that may reflect the ideals of one's childhood—that is, with Mexican associates, in a Mexican environment, and quite familistic. Status rewards are to be taken within a Mexican environment. Hence, such mobility might tend to expose the mobile person less to Anglos in work (even if it is middle-class work) and to less education (or possibly, to education inside the *barrio* context). Such people may, simply, not know how very much they resemble middle-class Anglo Americans in many values and attitudes. (The anxiety of such a Mexican American in a middle-class Anglo context cannot be ignored; he does not know the norms of sociability, and worries as much about proper behavior as a mobile person from any other ethnic group would.)

The second type of mobility is an experience that alienates Mexican Americans from other Mexican Americans. A typical pattern is that of dissociation from Mexican friends and schoolmates in high school in order to move increasingly in Anglo circles in high school, in college, and in work. It may end in anonymity and, perhaps, then a conscious decision for reidentification with Mexican Americans and even a conscious decision to enter or return to the *barrio*.

Intermarriage rates between Anglos and Mexican Americans give us some information on mobility (Table 6–2). Again, they emphasize the factors of time and place. From Table 6–2 it is evident that there has been a slowly increasing rate of intermarriage. It is also probable that the more "open" environments show more intermarriage at any given time. The Los Angeles material is presented in two ways: first, to show that generation affects intermarriage. In Los Angeles of 1963 the Mexican-born were the least likely of all Mexican Americans to marry Anglos. Children of Mexican parentage were the next most likely, and Mexican Americans with parents born in the United States were the most likely to marry Anglos. However, the Mexican born generation of Los Angeles is as likely as all Mexicans in San Antonio to marry outside the community. Second, Table 6–2 shows that in Los Angeles, persons with white collar occupations are far more likely to marry Anglos than are persons with lower-status occupations. White collar Mexicans are, of course, the most likely to mingle with Anglos. Moreover, for some upwardly mobile Mexicans, to marry an Anglo apparently has a symbolic value. (This is not to say there is no love and affection between the pair: mobility is simply an extra factor.) Thus intermarriage data shows that mobility may—or may not—mean assimilation. In a city like Los Angeles a mobile Mexican American can make a choice.

People with lower-status occupations also have options, though fewer than the middle class. Their situation also shows that change inside the Mexican American community is not a single process. In the cities many lower-class Mexicans also have residential options; but of course, in the cities more lower-class Mexicans than middle-class Mexicans live in the *barrios*. As shown in Chapter Four, their social profile is much like that of the poor of any ethnic group. Many are unemployed, and many depend on welfare and pension payments. Many are older people; many are foreign-born and poorly educated. Often households are headed by women, and even if not, family solidarity may not be enough to compensate for an endlessly unrewarding life. But the poor can show at least one kind of social mobility: they can change their circumstances by moving physically.

Geographical mobility is one of the two kinds of social mobility among Mexicans. If the social class system is considered as a set of ranks, the ethnic system can also be considered a set of ranks. It is mobility both to move into the middle class and to move inside the ranks of the ethnic

TABLE 6–2

ENDOGAMY RATES: PERCENT OF MEXICAN AMERICANS MARRYING WITHIN THE GROUP

City and Date	Endogamy Rates [a]
Albuquerque, 1929–1940	92
Los Angeles, 1924–1933	91
San Antonio, 1940–1955	90
Los Angeles, 1963	75
Albuquerque, 1964	81

	MA Grooms	MA Brides
Los Angeles, 1963: Mexican born	87	80
U.S. born of Mexican parents	77	74
U.S. born of U.S. parents	69	68
Los Angeles, 1963: high-status occupations	60	49
medium-status occupations	78	72
low-status occupations	79	80

Sources: Albuquerque, 1929–1940, derived from Carolyn Zeleny, "Relations between the Spanish-Americans and the Anglo-Americans in New Mexico" (Ph.D. dissertation, Yale University, 1944).

Los Angeles, 1924–1933, derived from Constantine Panunzio, "Intermarriage in Los Angeles, 1924–1933," *American Journal of Sociology,* XLVII (1942), 690–701.

San Antonio, 1940–1955, derived from Benjamin S. Bradshaw, "Some Demographic Aspects of Marriage" (M.A. thesis, University of Texas, 1960).

Los Angeles, 1963, from Frank G. Mittelbach and Joan W. Moore, "Ethnic Endogamy—the Case of Mexican Americans," *American Journal of Sociology,* LXXIV (July, 1968) 50–62.

Albuquerque, 1964, derived from Nancie L. González, *The Spanish Americans of New Mexico,* Advance Report 9 (Los Angeles: University of California, Mexican American Study Project, 1967).

[a] Rates are for *individuals.* If we had calculated rates on the base of marriages rather than persons, a higher proportion of *marriages* involving Mexican Americans would be exogamous, or with non-Mexicans.

system. It is social mobility as well as geographical mobility to move from Texas to Los Angeles, irrespective of social class. Thus mobility from the country to the city or from one state to another state is more important for Mexican Americans than even for Negroes. It may be meaningful even for those Mexicans who have accomplished nothing very substantial in the occupational world by the move. Even the occupationally unsuccessful know that such a move gives children much greater chances for occupational and income gains.

A move from one part of the Southwest to another is never easy. It is usually accomplished only after careful and long consideration and by use of a network of kinship relations and acquaintances. It can occur in youth as a sort of exploration of the world, or it can occur later with a family. Many of the movers return home: some miss the close relationships of the small town; others are badly trained and recognize their deficiencies in a more demanding area. (A college education can be of doubtful interchangeability in the Southwest: some colleges are of as poor quality as certain southern Negro colleges.) However, it should be noted that this radical shift in structures of opportunity can be accomplished by Mexican Americans without leaving the Southwest.

This availability of opportunity in different parts of the Southwest, particularly in southern California, plus the probable presence of friends and relatives in the new city may be the reason why so few Mexican Americans do leave the Southwest. A Mexican who leaves rural Texas for Los Angeles is spanning nearly the full range of opportunity available in this society.

CITIES AND THE CHANGING FAMILY

Familism seems to be declining in the big cities of the Southwest. Here again, the burden of certain family responsibilities is greatly diminished by public services available in the city. The city offers more jobs, temporary and permanent. Availability of welfare services diminishes the obligation to support an indigent relative. If a widowed or deserted wife does not *choose* to live with her relatives, she may do otherwise. Her choice may involve the personal degradation of bureaucratized Anglo charity, but it is still an option. That there are many who take such options is shown by the very few extended-family households in Los Angeles and San Antonio: very few Mexican Americans in these two cities will "double up" families even if so doing is supposed to be the "norm" of Mexican culture. Nearly all families in these two cities live in single-family households.[15]

In general, family roles change to meet changing circumstances. For urban Mexican American families it appears there has been more shift in the male role and role expectations than in the female role. (One sign of this lack of change in the female role is that female juvenile delinquency is notably lower than among other ethnic groups.)[16] Women

[15] See Grebler, et al, *The Mexican American People,* for data on generalizations made in this section.

[16] Joseph Eaton and Kenneth Polk, *Measuring Delinquency* (Pittsburgh: University of Pittsburgh Press, 1961) gives rates of delinquency by sex for Los Angeles juveniles of several ethnic groups.

still find their major role and validation in their families, as wives and especially as mothers. Higher education and careers are still alien to many Mexican American women. Even a working wife is considered an embarrassment by most Mexican American men.

It seems, however, that standards of behavior for men are shifting away from the patriarchal ideal to a norm of equality. Increasingly, Mexican American men are inclined to share important family decisions with their wives. In Los Angeles, Mexican American men are less embarrassed to care for children than the traditional norms suggest. Today they are considerably less in need of the subservient servant-like wife than the traditional norms suggest. Men in Albuquerque and San Antonio are more traditional than those in Los Angeles. This suggests that the changes in familism occur not simply because of a mass effect (television, for example) but rather because of the increased visibility of a variety of styles of intrafamily relationships that a city as large and as complex as Los Angeles offers. Importantly, husband and wife interaction is likely to become increasingly significant as the interaction between wife and female relatives and husband and male friends becomes less significant.

Middle-class norms remain the parental ideal for many Mexican American children. These may be Mexican middle-class norms, with emphasis on respect and deference to elders; American middle-class norms, with emphasis on getting along with other people and on getting ahead in the world; or some combination of the two. Although children are important and highly valued in the Mexican American family, an increasing proportion of Mexican Americans use and approve of birth control devices, despite their Catholicism. Thus, there may be in the future some notable reduction in the extremely high birth rate of this population. Nevertheless, important interregional and interclass differences will persist in regard to this issue; the isolated Mexican in parts of Texas is almost sure to remain traditionalistic for a longer time than others. The 1968 Papal Encyclical on birth control may also have an influence on the birth rate.

Extended family functions have declined, and with them there appears to have been a decline in *compadrazgo* in the cities. Nonetheless, among special subgroups of Mexican Americans, even in the large cities, it remains an important linking device. Political and civic activists have often found these alliances a convenience in formalizing chains of obligations among people who are not actual relatives. These bonds appear to be more like the bonds of "lodge brother" or "fraternity brother" than the tradition that a bond among *compadres* implies. Such an alliance may be even more necessary among minority politicians than among politicians in the larger society. Minority politicians rarely seem to have as many ties of mutual support, mutual aid, and information as do Anglo political and civic leaders.

Mexican Americans are largely second generation immigrants and children of the poorest peasant class from a very poor Latin-American nation. They have nearly always lived in highly segregated situations. These circumstances make the extent of change in family norms surprising. On the other hand, Mexicans often reject what they consider *gringo* norms when, in fact, they are rejecting *gringo* deviancy. Anglos in frequent contact with Mexican Americans are often surprised to be told that some ordinary facet of middle-class American values (careful supervision of young children, as one example) is "typically Mexican." "I always worry about my children when they're at school. That's typically Mexican, you know." Long isolation and the consequent ethnocentrism often makes Mexican Americans very anxious about their participation in American society and, quite often, poor informants about the features of Mexican family or individual norms that are truly distinctive.

Everybody in the Southwest thinks he knows something about the natural inclinations and habits of Mexican Americans. This overlay of preconceptions and stereotypes is the primary difficulty in understanding and even in studying Mexican American culture.

Ideally the professional training of the social scientist gives him the ability to see and to describe a matrix of culture without preconception, though this ideal is realized only now and then. The less disciplined observer, Anglo or Mexican, often sees what he wants to see, or generalizes wrongly from correct observation. He may be limited to what he sees in his job as social worker, teacher, or citrus grower; or the Mexican may be restricted by what he must tell the Anglo community in order to retain his status as spokesman and extract favors for the *barrio*. Thus Anglos and Mexicans in southwestern communities (and a certain amount of the scholarly literature) continue to perpetuate clearly formulated but often inconsistent and weakly substantiated ideas about Mexican American culture. Social and even personal values are rarely far below the surface. Sometimes the values are obvious and glaring.

Language and Culture

We must say flatly at the beginning of this chapter that there is very little firm systematic knowledge about what exists, none about why it exists; and any speculation about what *ought* to be should be left to the policy makers and to the people themselves. We have some solid information about the persistence of Spanish and good evidence that certain patterns of behavior and values do hold up (but rather inconsistently) across the variety of Mexican ethnic communities in the Southwest. Accordingly we will consider only those aspects of Mexican American culture on which some systematic and objective data are available: in regard to language, distinctive patterns of behavior and values, and the question of ethnic cohesiveness. Even so, the data are limited.

THE NATIVE LANGUAGE

No foreign language has been so persistently retained and is as likely to survive in this country as Spanish. This remarkable "language loyalty," or persistence, is attributable primarily to the Mexican Americans, according to a recent and extensive survey of language loyalty in the United States.[1] Surveys show that most Mexican Americans in Los Angeles, San Antonio, and Albuquerque are bilingual in Spanish and English. Some speak no English, and a small proportion speak no Spanish. This pattern is "normal" for American ethnic groups. Most of those speaking Spanish in Los Angeles and San Antonio were either Mexican-born or have Mexican-born parents. The special loyalty of Mexican Americans, however, appears when we see what a large proportion of Spanish speakers there are among New Mexican descendants of seventeenth century settlers and among third or more generation Mexicans in the border towns and in the more isolated areas of the other states. Mexican Americans speak Spanish not only to communicate with foreign-born relatives but habitually and as a matter of tradition through many generations. Why is this so?

Part of the answer lies in the special history of the isolated Mexican Americans of these special areas. Even today a visitor entering a small town in south Texas (Presidio, Rio Grande City, etc.) or a village in northern New Mexico or southern Colorado (Truchas, Tres Piedras) will hear Spanish rather than English as the normal language in the streets and shops. The few Anglos in many such towns are oftentimes also bilingual. Learning Spanish in these places is essential for social and economic survival, just as learning English is essential for Mexicans nearly anywhere else in the United States. In the previous generation all-Mexican work crews throughout the Southwest were supervised in Spanish—even in the large cities. Anglo bosses learned enough simple Spanish to handle the work situation. Thus Mexican families speaking only Spanish could go on living in a completely Spanish-speaking environment. This degree of isolation has fallen off sharply in most larger cities but it still may be found in, for example, the Los Angeles garment shops that employ recent immigrants as laborers. But it is very common in many rural areas of the Southwest and few except for those in school and perhaps young men who enter the Army need to speak any language except Spanish.

When Mexicans leave these villages and rural areas for the large cities they bring with them their language patterns. Thus the new arrival coming to Albuquerque from the northern part of New Mexico is as handicapped in English as the "greenhorn" fresh from Tijuana. Most southwestern cities have such a steady influx of Spanish-speaking new arrivals. If the new arrivals choose to live in the *barrio* they will find retail stores, gas stations, and banks with clerks who speak Spanish by preference. There are Spanish-language movie theaters, religious services

[1] Joshua Fishman, ed., *Language Loyalty in the United States* (The Hague: Mouton and Co., 1966).

(both Catholic and Protestant) and Spanish radio and television.[2] There are politicians and social workers ready to speak Spanish—for whom, in fact, an ability to speak Spanish can be an important part of their career.

Just as with some other ethnic groups in transition, the use of Spanish carries great symbolic meaning. This symbolism began from the time of the earliest contacts between Mexicans and Anglos. It is today widely believed that the right of Mexican Americans to use Spanish is guaranteed by the Treaty of Guadalupe Hidalgo. This is not true. It *is* true, however, that the constitution of the state of New Mexico, drawn up in 1912, guarantees that "the right of any citizen of the state to vote, hold office, or sit upon juries, shall never be restricted, abridged, or impaired on account of . . . inability to speak, read, or write in English or Spanish languages." [3] For years the state legislature of New Mexico was officially bilingual, with, of course, a certain liberty in translation adding to the political spice of the proceedings.

Thus the right to speak Spanish meant, symbolically, a certain inalienable right guaranteed to a conquered people. This symbol has gained in significance because the right to speak Spanish had been so suppressed by the public school system. In many parts of the Southwest children are still flatly forbidden to speak Spanish in school, both inside and outside the classroom; and apparently corporal punishment was used to enforce these regulations in some instance. "Spanish detention" (being kept after school for speaking Spanish) is still practiced in some schools.[4] Hence an anomalous situation, not conducive to learning, has been perpetuated: the use of Spanish in informal relationships persists along with the enforced use of English in formal situations.

Whatever the pedagogic reasons, the prohibition of Spanish has been a symbol of cultural suppression. Educational professions have, for a very long time, defined language problems as the major source of Mexican American troubles in school. Just as did their counterparts in the schools of the East generations ago, they often have used strong measures to bring about the desired change from Spanish to English. However, in the Southwest, these measures appear to have been largely ineffectual in an environment where work, street life, and leisure all were dominated by the use

2 In 1960, 66 percent of the total American foreign-language broadcasting and 86 percent of the foreign-language broadcasting in the West was in Spanish. Mary Ellen Warshauer, "Foreign Language Broadcasting," in Fishman, *Language Loyalty in the United States*, p. 80.

3 State Constitution of New Mexico, New Mexico Bluebook, 1921, Article VIII, Section 3, p. 21

4 Thomas Carter, "Mexican Americans in Schools," untitled study sponsored by the Mexican American Study Project, under a grant from the College Entrance Examination Board (Los Angeles: University of California). A revised version of the study will be published by the CEEB.

of Spanish. Much of this environment is now changing as Spanish-speaking parents slowly begin to interact more substantially with Anglo American society. A recent survey of school districts in California with a large proportion of Mexican American children showed that only 20 percent of those children needed an "English as a second language" program. (These included many small agricultural areas.) [5] In seven counties of south Texas, however, a huge 69 percent of the Spanish-surname students spoke little or no English when they entered school.[6]

Even more disturbing to many Mexican American intellectuals than the loss of Spanish through English-speaking schools is their awareness that the historical suppression of Spanish has tended to degrade the quality of the Spanish. Many of the immigrants to the United States were illiterate agricultural workers who spoke a variety of rural Spanish. Years of exposure to American society meant that English words were adapted to Spanish syntax. Common among every immigrant population, this mixture of language is called "interference." Interference in Spanish produces such neologisms (*pochismos*) as *el troque* (the truck), *la ganga* (the gang) and *huáchale* (Watch it!). In parts of Mexico near the border people often find themselves eating in *loncherias,* or in Los Angeles, perhaps, at a "Mexicatessen."

These words may amuse the Anglo but they are a source of deep embarrassment to many Mexican Americans, especially in their relationship with educated Mexican nationals. The Mexican American visiting Mexico as a tourist (such visits are increasingly common) is instantly recognized by his accent and by his use of *pochismos,* and is accordingly ridiculed. Spanish-language radio and television stations in the United States go to Latin American countries to recruit announcers. As one Texas radio station owner remarked, "I have tried to acquire the services of our local youth as Spanish announcers, but have found them to be unqualified to speak correctly the language left to them through heritage. It has been necessary for my station to import announcers." [7]

Pochismos are not only an indication of shift in a language but also a sure indication that Spanish is giving way to English. As one Mexican American lawyer in south Texas commented:

[5] Statement of Eugene Gonzáles, Assistant Superintendent of Public Instruction, California State Department of Education, in hearings before the Special Subcommittee on Bilingual Education of the Committee on Labor and Public Welfare, U.S. Senate, 90th Congress, First Session, Part 2. (Washington, D.C.: Government Printing Office, 1967), p. 473.

[6] Statement of Harold R. Dooley, Director, Valley Association for Superior Education, in *ibid.,* Part 1, May 29, 1967, p. 275.

[7] Statement of Arthur Thomas, Vice President and General Manager, Radio Station KUNO, Corpus Christi, Texas, in *ibid.,* p. 259.

> I am sad to see the Spanish language fading in the United States, southwestern part. I can see it fading everywhere in the homes, particularly in the higher bracket homes of lawyers and doctors and well-to-do businessmen and other professional people. I mean in formerly Spanish speaking homes . . . I think it's a deterioration of a language and I think it is a mistake. These kids simply are being reared today where they cannot speak Spanish. The problem there is that they cannot speak Spanish, not that they cannot speak English. That's no problem whatever. Now it is still a problem with the lower income brackets. English is still a problem, there. You have got to teach them English.[8]

Stories symbolizing the depreciation of the language are common. Mexican American intellectuals who know and love Spanish-language classics and the vital contemporary literature resent what they perceive to be the American preoccupation with French and German as the only "cultured" foreign languages. A frequent theme is that this "liability" of Mexicans should be turned into a national asset so that the United States will always have diplomatic and other personnel to serve in the 18 Spanish-speaking countries of Latin America and South America. But as far as integration into practical job-seeking America is concerned, speaking Spanish continues to be a handicap. Written tests in union apprenticeship programs, civil service jobs, and training for law enforcement agencies are in English. Even school I.Q. tests are in English.

Variations in attachment to Spanish reflect in yet another way the great diversity of the Mexican American population. Some of the disparities between school achievement in Texas and in California reflect the disappearance of a Spanish "environment" in California. Surveys of Los Angeles and San Antonio show that this is indeed the case when people were asked what language they used to speak to their children at home. The most striking result of this survey is the fact that only a minority of the Mexican American respondents in Los Angeles used Spanish exclusively at home with the children. Among families living in mixed Anglo and Mexican neighborhoods, exclusive (or even near-exclusive) use of Spanish is quite unusual.

The crucial role of language among Mexican Americans cannot be overestimated. As a man from Texas remarked, "In Texas the teacher beat you for using Spanish in school to remind you that you are an American. Your friends beat you after school to remind you that you are a Mexican." In Texas using English at home or in a *barrio* environment may be taken as a sign of ethnic disloyalty. Thus a young Mexican American VISTA volunteer working in San Antonio was deeply disturbed

8 Statement of Robert P. Sanchez, Attorney at Law, McAllen, Texas, in *ibid.,* p. 288.

when San Antonio teenagers abused him for his poor Spanish. In San Antonio poor Spanish was disloyalty; in his Los Angeles home it meant nothing.

Any evaluation of this persistence, positive or negative, is controversial. No other attribute of the Mexican American is so loaded with symbolic values and has such consequences. Even to set out the prevailing options and opinions is to be controversial.

It is not a good thing in the United States not to speak the language of the country. If for no other reason, it is very hard for a Mexican American with little English to get and hold a skilled job. Nor is it possible for him to contribute much to the American economic structure or to American society. On the other hand, it is good for the American economic structure and for American society to have many truly bilingual individuals. However, nobody is quite sure whether it is good for *individuals* to be bilingual. It may be that having to learn to read and write in English (with no formal training in Spanish) means that accomplishment in the American public school system is extremely difficult for many Mexican American children. On the other hand, it is nothing very unusual or damaging for American society (or any society) to have many people who are only monolingual. The loss of a particular language may mean that an individual is denied something of his cultural heritage. However, to retain this heritage, he may be hopelessly and completely denied certain other cultural heritages and economic opportunities.

We can only say that the speaking of Spanish persists. It persists partly because of the isolation of many Mexican Americans. The fact that Spanish persists in isolated areas is a positive result stemming from an otherwise undesirable situation. Thus any reasonable discussion of the persistence of Spanish must recognize immediately that any attribution of goodness or badness to the persistence of Spanish depends upon the interests of the observer. Mexican American scholars bewail the disappearance of Spanish "by force" in the public school systems of the Southwest. And yet the outstanding failure of the same school system, according to educators, is that enough Spanish persists to damage the accomplishments of many Mexican American school pupils. As a practical consequence, school districts throughout the Southwest are experimenting with bilingual education. Moreover, the *Chicano* movement (see Chapter Eight) with its emphasis on ethnic self-awareness may contribute to a resurgence of the use of Spanish among young middle-class people. Educators are also experimenting with new methods of teaching youngsters more effectively in English. In the face of all these contradictions the social scientist must be content to point out that the use of Spanish is declining among native-born Mexican Americans. It is used less in large cities in California than in small cities in Texas, and is tending to decline in use among middle-class Mexican Americans.

BEHAVIOR AND VALUES

Even to begin to discuss the touchy and value-loaded subject of Mexican American culture we must recognize that it is really two different things. There is first the highly visible surface of "Mexican culture": the quaintnesses and artifacts that can be seen by any visitor. But beneath the surface there are behavior patterns and values that are far more important. The existence and pervasiveness of some though not of all, are in great controversy. All are in some way empirically measurable.

The visible surface of Mexican American culture includes a great range of oddities. In Los Angeles, visitors are shown the shops of Olvera street; the famous Plaza, a popular tourist center, and a huge baroque church in downtown Los Angeles that is much used by Mexicans. There are distinctive modes of dress and hairstyles although these modes are often marks of specifically lower-class Mexicans. Occasionally a visitor may see a *curandera* (faith healer), and there are shops selling a variety of esoteric herbs for medicine. There are many foods peculiar to Mexicans and to Mexican restaurants. A special kind of music is played endlessly on southwestern Mexican radio stations. These are the interesting touches that a casual visitor can accept as "Mexican culture." They are a little touching, a little quaint, and often kept alive for commercial purposes in such tourist centers as Disneyland because they make money and please visitors.

This visible surface does not contradict the impressions gained from the rather restricted range of Mexican life available to the average Anglo's observation, because this range of Mexican life is structured by both social class and age. Thus, contact between Mexican Americans and Anglos may be at a maximum in youth, when both are in school. However, even this limited contact is likely to be structured by social class. The Anglo child who goes to a predominantly Mexican American school is likely to be relatively lower class. The Mexican going to a predominantly Anglo school is likely to be middle class. But given the proportions of each group in most southwestern cities, *most* Anglos probably will have little opportunity to interact extensively with Mexicans even in a school setting. This lack of opportunity would hold solely on the basis of probabilities, even if there were no other mechanisms of ethnic exclusiveness.

For adults, it is likely that most interethnic contacts between middle-class Anglos and Mexicans occur within an institutional context in which the Mexican is very likely to be lower class. Thus the Anglo professional working in public health, schools, welfare, probation, law enforcement and similar agencies "knows Mexicans" only when they are very young or in trouble. This fact may affect the general middle-class Anglo perception of the ingredients of Mexican culture, and may be as important as the fact that Mexicans are, of course, most frequently seen in clearly lower-class occupations.

This skewed nature of Mexican American and Anglo contact is almost surely an important influence on mutual perception. We can possibly summarize this off-balance perception by noting that most middle-class Mexicans are probably familiar with middle-class Anglos. Most middle-class Anglos don't know middle-class Mexicans. This lack of contact obviously can affect middle-class perception of the ingredients of Mexican culture.

Some of the cultural misunderstandings arising from institutional contacts have resulted in a special literature about Mexican Americans. In public health practice, to name one institutional area, the notable difficulty of getting Mexican cooperation has prompted considerable systematic research in areas beyond overt behavior. Some such studies into Mexican folk beliefs about the causes of illness are important and interesting. We note, for example, that several conditions Mexican Americans define as illness are not known or recognized by modern medicine. (Conversely, modern medical practice diagnoses certain conditions in a fashion totally discordant with folk beliefs.) One folk belief, in *susto* (fright), is closely related to the belief in Mexico that a soul can be jarred out of the body by terror, and illness will ensue. Another folk belief is that poor health may result from a mixture of a "hot" food (white beans, rice, fish, peppers) and a "cold" food (red beans, beef, cucumbers).[9] In New Mexico considerable research into such folk beliefs and folk diagnoses has led to a series of manuals for public health workers who may be called upon to deal with the folk diseases and diagnoses.

Whatever the degree of "superstition" or folk theory about illness, the observers are struck by the pragmatic quality with which illnesses are acted upon by Mexican Americans in remote areas. A visit to a folk healer may delay a visit to a doctor. Sometimes this places a seriously ill patient in danger, but at other times a minor ailment is cured at very low cost. Along with the folk healer and the herbalist, the poor make use of the supply of patent medicine in the local drugstore and the local public health clinic as well. Different levels of belief and of usage may exist in

[9] Good discussions of folk medicine appear in Margaret Clark, *Health in the Mexican American Culture* (Berkeley and Los Angeles; University of California Press, 1959), and Lyle Shannon, *Cultural Differences and Medical Care: The Case of the Spanish Speaking People of the Southwest* (New York: Russell Sage Foundation, 1954), as well as several of the community studies cited elsewhere in this book.

the same household. The mix of beliefs gets even more complex in metropolitan areas where the range of resources increases and the behavior of neighbors and friends about health becomes more varied. Perhaps more important, the local network of social relations and controls that accompanies a close group of neighbors and friends in a city permits more "strangers" to enter the system. Thus an individual may behave in more "deviant" fashion and go unpunished, or unobserved.

The decline of these "Mexican" health practices does much to illustrate the fate of some visible features of this special culture. In general, practices detrimental to welfare tend to disappear in a quite pragmatic fashion in urban areas. Some usages persist, perhaps because they are pleasant and quite harmless as, for example, the use of herbal teas. But in the past many mobile Mexican Americans felt it necessary to discard all such behavior. Some now prefer the drugstore patent medicines to "superstitions." It is increasingly likely that various levels of medical practices co-exist among the poor of less isolated areas.

Other visible cultural features suffer the same fate: conspicuously "Mexican" styles of dress are rejected along with the Spanish language, Mexican food, Mexican music, and Mexican folk religion. Interestingly, however, some of these things are being revived by the newer generation of middle-class mobile Mexicans. (Middle-class Mexican Americans in California universities enjoy wearing Pancho Villa-type mustaches, jeans, and boots. These are meaningful to the young, though often irritating to parents. The "natural" hair style might similarly disturb an older-generation member of the American black bourgeoisie.) Such self-conscious adoption of Mexican culture is still quite rare, although it is on the increase. There are upwardly mobile middle-class Mexican American families who collect pre-Columbian pottery, but the ordinary middle-class reaction is to reject such pottery as "primitive." Sometimes innocent middle-class Anglos assume that middle-class Mexicans are interested in Mexican art of Indian origin. The results can be embarrassing.

We also have some data on Mexican American familism. Mexican Americans are seen by Anglos and by themselves as particularly familistic (Chapter Six). That is, they place more value on family relations and obligations than do most Americans. In Chapter Six we suggested a possible function of familism in an economy of destitution. It was also suggested that no matter how familism might serve Mexican Americans as a group, there are certain ways in which it may be dysfunctional for Mexican American individuals and families. It may inhibit geographic mobility, perhaps preventing a move from being successful (there is some scattered evidence that this is a classic reason for Mexican Americans having difficulty in settling in a new location). It is also plain that familism is more dysfunc-

TABLE 7–1

PERCENT OF MEXICAN AMERICAN SURVEY RESPONDENTS
HOLDING FAMILISTIC VALUES, BY INCOME, LOS ANGELES,
SAN ANTONIO AND ALBUQUERQUE, 1965–1967

Value			Percent Agreeing with Item			
	1. Los Angeles					
	High Income		Medium Income		Low Income	
	Per-cent	Total N (=100%)	Per-cent	Total N (=100%)	Per-cent	Total N (=100%)
A. Immobility a	7	344	15	292	26	277
B. Nepotism b	22	353	36	292	41	272
	2. San Antonio					
			Medium Income		Low Income	
			Per-cent	Total N (=100%)	Per-cent	Total N (=100%)
A. Immobility a			15	317	35	239
B. Nepotism b			29	291	58	228
	3. Albuquerque					
	High Income		Medium Income		Low Income	
	Per-cent	Total N (=100%)	Per-cent	Total N (=100%)	Per-cent	Total N (=100%)
A. Immobility a	4	22	2	50	28	39
B. Nepotism b	4	22	6	50	28	39

Data for Los Angeles and San Antonio were provided courtesy the Mexican American Study Project, University of California at Los Angeles, and for Albuquerque by Operation SER, Santa Monica, California. All three surveys used probability samples of Mexican American households. Income levels vary greatly among the three cities, and, accordingly, different definitions of "high" "medium" and "low" have been applied, though each refers to approximately comparable levels of living. *Source for wording of items:* Joseph A. Kahl, "Some Measures of Achievement Orientation," *American Journal of Sociology,* LXX (May, 1965), 680–81.

a "When looking for a job, a person ought to find a position in a place located near his parents, even if that means losing a good opportunity elsewhere."

b "If you have the chance to hire an assistant in your work, it is always better to hire a relative than a stranger."

tional for society at large than for the individual. Familistic systems foster nepotism in business. In a familistic society such nepotism may not pose any real problem, but the United States is generally not directly nepotistic. It is a truism in American business that the family corporation dominated by the sons of the boss is likely to suffer more from competition or from corporate raiders. Many bosses recognize the situation and prefer to preserve the family firm by hiring a good management team using the famed methods of the Harvard Business School. Nepotism may not be important for a tiny shop in a Mexican American community, but familistic ethnic groups will have to adopt the business practices of the larger society if they are to succeed in it.

These are speculations, but some evidence is available on the extent to which the values of immobility and nepotism are held by Mexican Americans in Los Angeles, San Antonio, and Albuquerque. We also know something about what kind of Mexicans hold these values. (Table 7–1.) It must be remembered that many of these people have either moved themselves or are the children of persons who moved from smaller towns and rural areas (or from Mexico) to one of these three urban areas; thus they are the more mobile ones. Therefore it should not be too surprising to find that very few Mexican Americans agree (as phrased in the question on the survey) that "a person should . . . locate near his parents" when he is looking for a job, even if it means losing a good job. Many of these individuals have, in fact, done just that by moving away from their community of birth. But the difference in the value given familism by Mexicans of differing income levels is notable, irrespective of what city they live in.

Almost no higher-income persons in any city agree with the statement of familism; only a small minority of even the very poor in any city agree with the statement.

Nepotism is a different story. A higher proportion (even a slight majority of the poor in San Antonio) believe "it is better to hire a relative than a stranger." The tendency to agree with this response is much lower among the more well-to-do in each city. This suggests that those who are doing reasonably well are indeed more acculturated to the values of American society about nepotistic hiring. They are more likely to hold jobs in companies that promote competitive values quite explicitly, because they are less likely to be in "dead-end" jobs where promotions are rarely achieved. (Promotable jobs mean an emphasis on competition. For Mexicans, few of whom have fathers who own the business, these provide true competition.) Differences between cities are notable, as well as differences between groups of Mexicans by income. Mexicans in San Antonio hold most firmly to nepotistic values; those in Los Angeles are next; and those in Albuquerque are last. Though the direct relationship is not clear, it may be significant that the Albuquerque sample were almost all Spanish Americans who have lived in the United States for many generations; respondents in the other two cities include many more Mexican immigrants and the children of Mexican immigrants. We can surmise, therefore, that these two broad values attached to familism are considerably less important to Mexican Americans than either they or the larger society generally believe.

Among many other features of the Mexican value system that are said to be different from Anglo American norms, it is said that Mexicans emphasize the present rather than the future, intangible gratifications rather than material rewards, and emphasize enjoyment rather than (from one Anglo interview) the "run-run-run" of other Americans. The Mexican is pictured as a serene rather than an anxious person, perhaps just a bit improvident in planning for the future, but his pleasure in life and living more than compensates.

The temptation, of course, is to say that this is just a romantic projection. In fact, few systematic sources provide evidence for such an attitude among Mexican Americans. The most important of these is the Kluckhohn study of a small village in New Mexico.[10] Even in this small village Florence Kluckhohn noted substantial change in a comparatively short time in the basic value preference pattern. She predicted that acculturation to the dominant value system of American society would probably occur for most of the villagers as they became more integrated into the institutions (particularly economic) of the larger American society.

These values are as clearly expressed in this remote New Mexican village study as anywhere in the literature. Before we consider them as totally opposite in usefulness to the values of modern American society, it is worth remembering that such values are generally integrated with—and functional in—the environment in which people live. The pace of change of society and technology is very slow in a remote village. The slow change of seasons and the natural risks of any agricultural society may mean that American urban values may not be useful in a small New Mexican village. And of course, a present-time orientation is not the only alternative to a future-time orientation. One can venerate the past (as is done in New Mexico) and *still* plan for the future. Subjugation to nature is not the only alternative to mastery over nature; one can feel in harmony with natural forces rather than at their mercy.[11] But to plan meaningfully for the future in a small mountain village with a primitive technology might mean a kind of insanity or even an alienation so complete that such an individual could not cope with the realities of the environment and

[10] See Florence R. Kluckhohn and Fred L. Strodtbeck, *Variations in Value Orientations* (Evanston, Ill. and Elmsford, N.Y.: Row, Peterson and Co., 1961).

[11] It was Kluckhohn who found Spanish Americans of New Mexico to be more present-oriented than future-oriented and to see man more as subjugated to nature than as master over nature. In both cases, the latter is the pattern of the dominant American culture.

would ultimately emigrate. In fact, there *is* a great deal of emigration—enough to leave some of these villages nearly depopulated. Whatever these speculations one can argue in retrospect that traditional values, at least at a time in the past, may very well have been of adaptive value to Mexican American communities.

Our data on these values as held in urban environments is limited, but we do have some information (Table 7–2) from Los Angeles, San Antonio, and Albuquerque. These data show, for example, the strong relationship between reaction to traditional values and the income of the individual. The poor in all three cities are far more traditional. *Most* poor Mexican Americans see comparatively little virtue in planning because "plans are hard to fulfill." *Most* poor Mexican Americans try to "be content with what comes their way," rather than "expecting too much out of life." But, interestingly, comparatively few at any income level are wholeheartedly in favor of "thinking only about the present, without worrying about what is going to happen tomorrow." Apparently, even if you distrust planning for the future, it is wise at least to *worry* about the future. When we look for differences between the three cities we see (as with familism) that the middle-class Spanish Americans of Albuquerque are the most "acculturated" about these values.

What do these findings imply? They certainly suggest that cultural value patterns are highly responsive to the demands of a situation. Some comparable data from Anglo Americans in New Mexico suggests that middle-class Mexican Americans and Anglos respond *almost identically* to all of the items in both tables. The poor Mexicans are far more traditional than the poor Anglos. This is extremely interesting, suggesting as it does that poor Mexican Americans, many from small villages, tend to follow village patterns of values even after they have moved to the cities. It may imply that the poor Mexican American must change much more in order to adapt to an industrial and urban environment than must the poor Anglo Americans. It may imply that the children of poor Mexican Americans are more easily discouraged from planning related to schooling than are the children of poor Anglos. It is risky to draw too many inferences from just a few questions, but the problem of finding adequate evidence on urban patterns of cultural retention and cultural change is very great. It is very probable that lower-class Mexican American school problems and work problems are related to these underlying patterns of values. It is reasonable on the basis of the available evidence to suggest that these patterns add up to an easy discouragement—and a tendency to fall back on family, friends, and the familiar ways of the past rather than to struggle with a new and alien environment.

Mexican Americans are reputed to be clannish. "They stick together.

TABLE 7–2

PERCENT OF MEXICAN AMERICAN SURVEY RESPONDENTS
HOLDING TRADITIONAL VALUES, BY INCOME
LOS ANGELES, SAN ANTONIO AND ALBUQUERQUE, 1965–1967

Value						
			Percent Agreeing with Item			

1. Los Angeles

	High Income		Medium Income		Low Income	
	Per-cent	Total N (= 100%)	Per-cent	Total N (= 100%)	Per-cent	Total N (= 100%)
a. Don't plan a	35	359	49	285	63	268
b. Think present b	26	354	24	290	35	261
c. Be content c	56	359	73	290	80	271

2. San Antonio

	Medium Income		Low Income	
	Per-cent	Total N (= 100%)	Per-cent	Total N (= 100%)
a. Don't plan a	46	316	58	242
b. Think present b	17	307	38	248
c. Be content c	59	312	69	245

3. Albuquerque

	High Income		Medium Income		Low Income	
	Per-cent	Total N (= 100%)	Per-cent	Total N (= 100%)	Per-cent	Total N (= 100%)
a. Don't plan a	14	22	36	50	62	39
b. Think present b	14	22	18	50	49	39
c. Be content c	32	22	69	50	69	39

See Table 7–1 for sources of data.

Source for wording of items: Joseph A. Kahl, "Some Measures of Achievement Orientation," *American Journal of Sociology,* LXX (May, 1965), 680–81.

a "Making plans only brings unhappiness because the plans are hard to fulfill."

b "With things as they are today, an intelligent person ought to think only about the present, without worrying about what is going to happen tomorrow."

c "The secret of happiness is not expecting too much out of life, and being content with what comes your way."

They don't want anything to do with other Americans." From available historical material (Chapter Two) we know that such clannishness in the past was often imposed upon Mexicans by their strict isolation from American society. Such isolation occurred because of settlement patterns and work patterns and was retained or reinforced by many Anglo institutions. Isolation is hardly avoidable in a town where Mexicans must attend segregated schools, work in segregated industries, and live in segregated residential areas. Thus, "clannishness" was inevitable and oftentimes it would be exacerbated by open prejudice, discrimination, and in some cases, the state of open conflict between Mexican nationals and the United States.

Clannishness is an important defense for a poor and unskilled population in a demanding, indifferent, or hostile environment. Some of this attitude is a natural consequence of Mexican familism: a network of obligations was extremely important in the past among Mexican Americans and is important even today. In some ways the ethnic collectivity, that is, all Mexicans, functions as a more elaborate extension of the family. One is born into being Mexican and cannot escape the collective fate of all Mexicans. From this sense of group identification comes the term "ethclass," coined by Milton Gordon to describe the notion that an American is defined in social terms largely by a combination of his social class and his ethnicity or religious heritage. It assumes that the American Catholic, Jew, Negro, Puerto Rican, or Mexican American (and even the WASP) will generally prefer and/or be forced into social and occupational associations with fellow ethnics of his own class level.[12] In our discussion of social class (Chapter Six) we suggest that the extent of ethnic exclusiveness at various class levels varies with the nature of the local milieu. We used the terms "Frontier" and "Colony" to refer respectively to the more assimilationist and the more ethnically exclusive Mexican Americans. The proportion of Frontiersmen and Colonists varies from class to class and from city to city, depending upon a variety of factors. That the ethnically exclusive Colonists are more visible to the non-ethnic than are the Frontiersmen or assimilationists should not blind us to the fact that *both* types of adaptations exist.

For some ethnic groups there have appeared in-group terms referring to ethnic solidarity. The terms describe the sense of peoplehood, of a common history, of a sharing of common perceptions and preferences about the social world. "Soul brothers" for Negroes is such a term. For Mexican Americans the term is *la raza*. The word can be narrowly translated as "race," but its implications are far more complex than that among Mexican Americans and indeed among Latin Americans generally. Originally it referred to the creation of *la raza* in the fusion of the Spanish and the indigenous peoples of the New World. In fact, throughout Latin America Columbus Day is called *"El día de la Raza"*—the day of

12 See Milton M. Gordon, *Assimilation in American Life* (New York: Oxford University Press, 1964).

FIGURE 7–1

PERCENT OF MEXICAN AMERICANS HAVING
ALL MEXICAN AMERICAN ASSOCIATES [a]

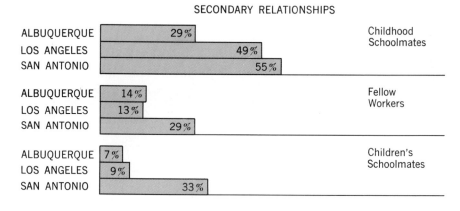

SECONDARY RELATIONSHIPS

ALBUQUERQUE	29%	Childhood Schoolmates
LOS ANGELES	49%	
SAN ANTONIO	55%	
ALBUQUERQUE	14%	Fellow Workers
LOS ANGELES	13%	
SAN ANTONIO	29%	
ALBUQUERQUE	7%	Children's Schoolmates
LOS ANGELES	9%	
SAN ANTONIO	33%	

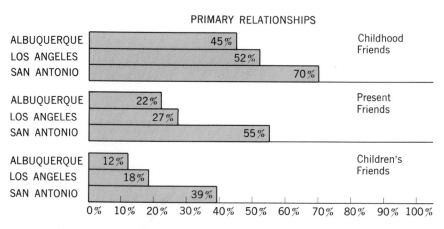

PRIMARY RELATIONSHIPS

ALBUQUERQUE	45%	Childhood Friends
LOS ANGELES	52%	
SAN ANTONIO	70%	
ALBUQUERQUE	22%	Present Friends
LOS ANGELES	27%	
SAN ANTONIO	55%	
ALBUQUERQUE	12%	Children's Friends
LOS ANGELES	18%	
SAN ANTONIO	39%	

0% 10% 20% 30% 40% 50% 60% 70% 80% 90% 100%

[a] Data from Los Angeles and San Antonio were provided by Mexican American Study Project, University of California, Los Angeles. Data from Albuquerque provided by Operation SER, Santa Monica, California.

la raza. Used among Mexican Americans, however, it appears to be restricted to fellow Mexican Americans. (This appears to be the case among all except the most militant, who attempt to include non-Mexican Latins.) A man accepting a federal appointment may state that, among other things, his new position will give him the opportunity to "do something for" (or he is accused by others of not doing something for) *la raza*. A similar term, although used somewhat differently, is the word *Chicano*.

Of obscure origin, it originally appears to have been a diminutive for the descriptive term *Mexicano*. The word now has in-group connotations. Mexican Americans tell one another that the clerk named Mrs. Smith is a *Chicana* and she'll help you out. *A lo Chicano* or *Chicano*-style refers to behavior that may range from a distinctive posture when driving a car to a distinctive set of manners and behavior used among proper Mexicans. The *Chicano* movement is the name given to the new politics (Chapter Eight) among Mexican Americans today.

We would not expect loyalty to *la raza* to decline in the modern social world of the United States, and there is no evidence that it has done so. Appeals to such loyalty are fully legitimate: there are very few people inside or outside the group who can comfortably sneer at such a form of clannishness, at least if it is on behalf of Mexican Americans. On the other hand, we find that ethnic exclusiveness in social relations is becoming far more variable. As noted in Chapter Six, intermarriage is increasing in Los Angeles, and this increase reflects the general growth in effective interaction with individuals outside the ordinary circle of Mexican Americans in work and friendship. In Chapter Six we presented data (Table 6–1) on how closely Mexican Americans in three important cities confine themselves to work and friendship with other Mexican Americans. There are striking differences between the three cities, and also between age groups, with, for example, 70 percent of the San Antonians and 55 percent of the Angelenos over 50 reporting that *all* their childhood schoolmates were Mexican, whereas 50 percent of the San Antonians and 42 percent of the Angelenos under 30 reported such ethnic exclusiveness in their childhood.

Even more interesting than the age differences, however, are what we might call generational differences. Figure 7–1 shows data for three cities for a study in which the respondents were asked how "Mexican" were their social relations during their childhoods, in the present, and for their own children. Thus, through one respondent we get a look at three generations. The figure also distinguishes between "primary" rela-tionships—friendships—and "secondary" relationships, those at school and at work. Of course, the city differences are of major importance, but even in such a segregated city as San Antonio the degree of "Mexican exclu-siveness" generally declines from one generation to the next.

However, it is important to note that leaving the fairly narrow circle of ethnic exclusiveness does not mean assimilation, and as a matter of fact, in some circles the word assimilation itself has become pejorative. It means, simply, that Mexican Americans have more options, less com-pulsion to confine relationships to fellow Mexican Americans either because of Anglo hostility or because of pressure from the ethnic community. One can help one's fellow Mexicans and retain full loyalty to ethnic traditions without total exclusiveness in social relations. To project a bit, it seems that the Mexican Americans living in ethnic frontiers appear to have made this decision for themselves. A few, but only a few, reject the name "Mexican American," preferring to be called simply "Americans." It also appears that some kind of "dualism" is emerging, to borrow a term common among Negroes at the turn of the century. Applied to Mexican Americans it expresses the idea that "we Mexicans are Americans but we also share the fate of all Mexicans."

❧ This dualism has been slow to appear. Many Mexican Americans believe themselves to be far more Mexican than American, a belief that is shaken by the disrespect and displacement they experience while visiting Mexico. Sometimes this belief is also helped along by Mexican American leaders and spokesmen who can reinforce their own position, that is, their basis of support, their "clientle," as Mexican American. There may be some echo of the black protest movement in the *barrios* in the recent demands by young intellectual Mexicans (as in Los Angeles) for courses in Mexican history, a demand matching perfectly the Negro interest in courses in African history. Some Mexicans want courses in Mexican American history and experience in the United States. How many of the demands will be met, how widespread the Mexican side of the dualism—answers to these questions depend upon subtle shifts in the internal meaning of being "Mexican" in modern American society. ❧

The political development of Mexican Americans can be traced through roughly four periods of political activity that begin with the American conquest of the Southwest.

Such a survey must begin with conflict. Though the first three generations of American rule (from the late 1840s until about 1920, the first phase of political development for Mexican Americans) can be termed "apolitical," it is a period that covers widely disparate activities. Through the first generation (until perhaps the mid-1870s) there was widespread violence and disorder accompanying the consolidation of the conquest. In the following 50 years throughout most of the Southwest Mexican Americans were politically submerged. Neither the violence of the first generation nor the quiescence of the second and third can be considered "normal" American political participation. Force and its aftermath of suppression were the rule.

Perspective on Politics

There were two exceptions to the dominant apolitical pattern. Organized political activity was very much present in New Mexico. Here the political system, even during the long period of territorial government, reflected the demographic and social weight of a large Spanish-speaking population. In southern California, moreover, a wealthy land-owning group of Mexicans retained substantial, although declining, political power until the late 1880s and the coming of the railroads.

In the second period, what may be considered conventional political activity began, born in a context of violence and suppression. This period (beginning roughly in the 1920s) was a time of adaptation and accommodation, reflecting the changing position of Mexican Americans in the social structure of communities in the Southwest. A small Mexican American middle class began to gain some strength and tried to come to terms politically with a still hostile and still threatening social environment.

This period of accommodation was typified by the efforts of the new Mexican American groups to prepare and to "guide" the lower-class and newly arrived immigrant Mexican Americans to "become Americans." Notably, they did *not* press for full political participation. As we shall see, it was also during this period that at least some of the negative ideological

Alfredo Cuéllar, author of Chapter Eight, "Perspective on Politics," is a PhD candidate at the University of California at Los Angeles.

assumptions about Mexicans held by the majority were reflected in their political activity.

The third period, beginning in the 1940s, saw increased political activity. Although the results fell far short of full participation in American political life, this period was characterized by a more aggressive style and more organization. During this time, so to speak, the Mexican Americans began to "play the game" according to Anglo political rules. The new idea of progress became associated with exercising the franchise and attempting to gain both elective and appointive office. The political achievements of Mexican Americans in New Mexico exemplified political progress. There, they had kept a political voice through the change from Mexican to U.S. rule: there were Mexicans in the state legislature and in Congress. Most areas, however, fell short of the accomplishment in New Mexico, especially south Texas, where political exclusion and manipulation were the heritage of violence and suppression. This exclusion and manipulation continued in many communities to be enforced by the local Anglo power structure.

The new aggressiveness that appeared after World War II was largely a phenomenon of urban life and reflected again the changing situation of Mexican Americans. They were becoming more urbanized, and more were middle class; they were increasingly American-born. World War II itself was one of the most important forces for change: hundreds of thousands of Mexican Americans served in the armed forces and gained radically new experiences, being sent outside their five-state *"barrio"* and given opportunities to develop a drastically changed view of American society.

⌐ In recent years a fourth type of political activity is becoming important. For convenience, it may be called the radicalization of Mexican American political activity. This new style is exemplified in the growth of the *Chicano* movement. Although this movement assumes different forms in various parts of the Southwest and although its acceptance is far from uniform, it is a very different concept of political activity. It questions and challenges not only the assumptions of other generations of Mexican American political leaders but some of the most basic assumptions of American politics as well.⌐

These four phases are roughly sequential, as noted in this outline, but they also overlap a good deal. Violence continues to suppress Mexican American political activity in many communities and to foster an apolitical attitude. In other areas there is a tentative and fearful kind of accommodation politics. Conventional political activity is slowly bringing a quite new political visibility to the Mexican Americans, which is particularly evident in Washington with the recent creation of the Inter-agency Committee on Mexican American Affairs. Radical politics is also becoming institutionalized in some parts of the Southwest. Despite this confusing and complex overlapping and coexistence, we will discuss each type of political activity separately.

CONFLICT AND APOLITICS

Conflict between Mexicans and Anglo Americans characterized the American Southwest for the better part of the nineteenth century.[1] Let us recall some of the history of the region with specific reference to its political consequences. (See Chapters Two and Three for a more general historical treatment.) The first sizeable number of Anglos who entered this region settled in Texas in 1821 under the leadership of Stephen Austin. Alarmed by their rapid increase in numbers and their failure to accept Mexican law and custom, the Mexican government shut off further Anglo immigration in 1830. The end result was the Texas Revolution of 1835–1836, just 15 years after the first legal immigration began. In spite of the Texas declaration of independence from Mexico, there were then 10 years of sporadic warfare, culminating in open warfare between the United States and Mexico in 1846 after the annexation of Texas by the United States.

The Treaty of Guadalupe Hidalgo ended the declared war, but it did not end the fighting between Mexicans and Anglos. Even in New Mexico, acquired "bloodlessly," an abortive rebellion followed the American occupation. In Texas, the next generation lived through an almost endless series of clashes, which reached the status of international warfare again in the late 1850s. Mexico's defeat and the humiliating invasion she suffered cost her nearly a third of her territory. For years afterward elements in Mexico dreamed of reconquest. On the American side the new territories were vast and remote from the central forces of government. The feeble hold that the United States had on the Southwest, the recurrent fears of Indian rebellion, and the divisive forces unleashed by the Civil War were all reflected in American fears of reconquest. Today, with the United States stretching from sea to sea, we rarely question the inevitability of this pattern. But a hundred-odd years ago, this "Manifest Destiny" had something of the character of a crusade, a national mission to be accomplished despite the acknowledged existence of great obstacles.

[1] The historical material in this chapter is drawn heavily from the historical source materials cited in Chapters Two and Three, and also on Walter Prescott Webb, *The Texas Rangers: A Century of Frontier Defense* (Boston: Houghton Mifflin Co., 1935), and on Ralph Guzmán, "The Political Socialization of the Mexican American People" (unpublished manuscript, 1967).

In this climate of opinion, defeating Mexico was a very special victory, and holding these territories a special cause.

Anglos used force to gain control, and Mexicans retaliated with force. Texas, the scene of virtually all of this activity and the home of most Mexicans resident in the United States, saw hostilities between substantial armies and a nearly constant state of guerilla warfare. Many Mexicans, perhaps the most dissident, chose to return to Mexico. From the Texas point of view, many of those who remained were ready as always to join any successful marauder from across the border.

Of these, the most successful was Juan Cortina, who first invaded Texas in 1859 in a series of skirmishes known now as the Cortina Wars. These long "wars" illustrate many of the important themes in Texas-Mexican-American history, showing the comparative lack of distinction between "Mexican" and "Mexican American." They illustrate the racial nature of the conflicts, and they also show that these early decades of conflict were inextricably linked with some larger American problems, most notably the Civil War.

The changes in the Texas economy during this period were detailed in (Chapter Two). It should be reiterated that the shift in land use entailed a shift in ownership. Often, political promises were made and broken; legal contracts were made and broken; legal protection for Mexicans—landowners and others—was promised and withheld. As Webb concludes in his history of the Texas Rangers, "The humble Mexicans doubted a government that would not protect their person and the higher classes distrusted one that would not safeguard their property. Here, indeed, was the rich soil in which to plant the seed of revolution and race war." [2]

Juan Cortina's expeditions began as a personal vendetta in Brownsville, Texas against an Anglo sheriff who used unnecessary force in arresting one of Cortina's former ranchhands. Cortina soon extended his campaign to a call for the general emancipation of Mexicans from American rule. He exhorted Mexicans to rise against their oppressors, to claim their lands and to drive out the *gringos*. Mexicans on both sides of the Rio Grande flocked to his camp. His army engaged troops in Texas in numerous battles, although eventually he and his army were forced to retreat into Mexico.

A few years later, after the Civil War, Cortina "helped" U.S. federal troops in the skirmishes and military occupation that preceded Reconstruction, an act that confirmed his unpopularity among Texas Anglos. Cortina went on to become brigadier general in the Mexican army and

2 Webb, *Texas Rangers,* p. 176.

later, governor of the border state of Tamaulipas in northern Mexico. But as late as the middle of the 1870s he was still leading raids into Texas.

Hundreds of other leaders led groups ranging from the pseudo-military to the simple bandit (though Mexicans often viewed such bandits as *guerilleros* fighting for their people). In California, "outlaws" such as Tiburcio Vásquez and Joaquín Murieta (the latter so romanticized that it is difficult to separate fact from fantasy) and in Texas, Juan Flores Salinas, were variously remembered by Anglos anxious for law and order and by Mexicans unwilling to recognize the legitimacy of the American regime. A monument to Salinas was erected in 1875 and carries the inscription: *que combatiendo murió por su patria* ("who died fighting for his country").

The end of the Civil War, however, released troops for the "pacification" of the southwestern Indians, and the railroads could bring in hordes of Easterners looking for land and a new frontier. The era of overt violence between Anglo and Mexican American came to an end and was followed by a long period of quiet. With the beginning of revolution in Mexico in 1910 came the beginning of large-scale immigration. This process rekindled the historical distrust of Mexican Americans, especially now that their numbers were being rapidly increased by refugees from Mexico. It was therefore not surprising that this process would have a depressive effect on political participation among Mexican Americans at this time.

There seemed always to be incidents to keep the Americans fearful. In 1915, for example, a Mexican agent was arrested in a Texas border city with a detailed "Plan de San Diego, Texas," for an insurrection in the Southwest in which "all Anglos over the age of 16 would be put to death." Bandit activities in Texas were being carried out to finance the revolutionary plans of the Flores Magon brothers, who were then operating out of Los Angeles in an effort to begin yet another revolution in Mexico. I.W.W. and anarchist activities among the Mexicans added to the anxiety. Then, in 1916 General Pancho Villa climaxed a number of border raids with an attack on Columbus, New Mexico. The United States retaliated with the Punitive Expedition of General John Pershing into northern Mexico. This comic-opera rerun of the tragic war with Mexico 70 years earlier increased distrust and resentment toward the Mexican American population. Then came the famous Zimmerman Note of 1917, which appeared to confirm all suspicions: the Germans offered to unite Mexico and Japan with Germany for a war against the United States to restore the Southwest to Mexico and give the Far West to Japan. Mexico showed no interest in the scheme, but it touched a sensitive nerve in the United States. As usual, the Mexican Americans in the Southwest were caught in the middle.

Given the background of distrust and violent suppression it is not surprising that the style of the first important Mexican American political groups should have been very circumspect. They could not have been anything but accommodationist.

THE POLITICS OF ADAPTATION

The politics of accommodation can be traced from the 1920s with the appearance of several new political organizations. A good example was the *Orden Hijos de America* (Order of the Sons of America), founded in San Antonio in 1921.[3] The founding members came almost entirely from the newly emerging middle class. Apparently, though, a few refugees from the Mexican Revolution were also involved. More important, both the social and the economic position of these founding members were precarious, and one can note in their announced objectives important concessions to the Anglo definition of the proper role for Mexicans in politics. For example, the goals of the OSA did *not* include demands for equality, either between Mexican Americans themselves or in terms of the dominant majority. Thus, only "citizens of the U.S. of Mexican or Spanish extraction, either native or naturalized" were eligible to join.[4] This exclusion by citizenship was meant—and acted—as an exclusionary mechanism. The implication was that Mexican Americans were more trustworthy to Anglos than Mexican nationals, and also more deserving of the benefits of American life.

This can be understood partly as a reaction to the Anglo conception of Mexicans as an undifferentiated group of low status, regardless of social achievement or citizenship. Hence, all were equally to be distrusted. As an organization of upwardly mobile individuals (albeit of modest achievements) OSA was concerned to show the dominant Anglo majority that they were different from other, "trouble-making" Mexicans. Of course citizenship would have been functionally useful if the *Orden* had been a truly political group, but the symbolic meaning of the requirement is

[3] This section draws heavily on Guzmán, "Political Socialization." See also Miguel D. Tirado, "Mexican American Community Political Organization" (unpublished manuscript in files of Ralph Guzmán, University of California Santa Cruz, 1969), and Robert A. Cuéllar, "A Social and Political History of the Mexican-American Population of Texas, 1929–1963" (unpublished Master's thesis, North Texas State University, Denton, Texas, 1969).

[4] Article III, constitution of OSA, cited by O. Douglas Weeks, "The League of United Latin-American Citizens," *The Southwestern Political and Social Science Quarterly*, X (December 1929), p. 260, cited in Tirado, "Mexican American Political Organization," p. 5.

indicated by another regulation. The organization declared itself "to assume no partisan stand, but rather to confine itself to training members for citizenship."

Obviously, "training members for citizenship" is not a strong political position, although presumably this included some activities aimed at increasing political participation, such as by voting. In general, though, this adaptive position could be interpreted as a reflection of the great social and economic vulnerability of Mexican Americans during the 1920s. Validation and recognition meant being as noncontroversial as possible— and preferably with declarations of loyalty to the United States of America.

OSA functioned for nearly ten years. By that time some splintering had begun to occur in the group and its chapters, and on February 17, 1929, several Mexican American groups, among them the OSA itself, the Order of Knights of America, and the League of Latin American Citizens, met in Corpus Christi, Texas. Out of this meeting a new organization emerged to meet the need for harmony and to present a unified front to the Anglo American community. The theme of unity was embodied in the name of the new organization: the League of United Latin-American Citizens, or LULAC. Once again, membership was restricted to citizens of Mexican or Spanish extraction, one of the group's aims being "to develop within the members of our race the best, purest and most perfect type of a true and loyal citizen of the United States of America." [5]

This obvious sensitivity to Anglo opinion was intensified by the debate in Congress and in the press at the time concerning the rising tide of Mexican immigration. This affirmation of loyalty and citizenship may therefore be interpreted as one further example of a protective device used by middle-class Mexican Americans vis-à-vis the Anglo society.

Thus in 1929, to protect themselves from social and economic sanctions, the willingness of Mexican Americans to assert even minimum political demands was tempered at all times and in all expressions by a desire to reaffirm citizenship and loyalty to the United States. It is not surprising that there was at this time no pressure for Mexican civil rights, particularly if it might have involved any kind of open demonstrations. (As a matter of fact, Article 1 of the LULAC's by-laws contains one item that states, "We shall oppose any radical and violent demonstration which may tend to create conflicts and disturb the peace and tranquility of our country.") Once again, a statement designed to appease, to reassure those Anglos who feared the worst. And it also served as a warning to Mexicans who might conceivably entertain such radical notions.

Notable by its omission among 25 articles is any demand for any

5 Weeks, "League," p. 260, cited in Guzmán, "Political Socialization," p. 355.

form of cultural pluralism, despite the willingness of some members to preserve a semblance of their ethnic identity.

Throughout, the aims and purposes of the new organization reflected its middle-class orientation, a conformity to the standards of Texas Anglo society, and above all, an emphasis on adapting to American society, instead of emphasis on aggressive political participation, and much less on any kind of political participation based on a separate ethnic identity.

Such circumspection must, as we have noted earlier, be judged in the context of the political milieu of Texas in the 1920s. Both Mexicans and Negroes "knew their place." Although Mexicans did vote in Texas, in some counties the votes were under the control of an Anglo political boss.[6] In other counties Mexicans seldom voted because of the poll tax and other such limitations. The influence of the Anglo *patrón* may be seen in the following letter written by one such boss, who felt it necessary to scold his "Mexican-Texas friends" for forming such a group as LULAC:

> I have been and still consider myself as your Leader or Superior Chief... I have always sheltered in my soul the most pure tenderness for the Mexican-Texas race and have watched over your interests to the best of my ability and knowledge.... Therefore I disapprove the political activity of groups which have no other object than to organize Mexican-Texas voters into political groups for guidance by other leaders.... I have been able to maintain the Democratic Party in power with the aid of my Mexican-Texas friends, and in all the time that has passed we have had no need for clubs or political organizations.[7]

Between hostility and economic vulnerability Mexican Americans were making the best of a difficult situation, which was very slow to change. LULAC gained power among the middle class and ultimately became a spokesman for those Mexican Americans who had achieved a measure of economic and social advancement. In Texas it is still an important political group. Other organizations (as well as branch chapters of LULAC) appeared throughout the Southwest, and many were modeled after LULAC. All of them skirted the question of aggressive political action with considerable skill. Accommodation was the style in the 1920s and 1930s; it may very well have been the only possible style. Since World War II LULAC has taken a much more aggressive stance, a change

---

[6] Mexican American voting was "managed," in V.O. Key's term. For a specific discussion of Texas Mexican American politics see his *Southern Politics* (New York: Vintage edition, Alfred A. Knopf, Inc., 1949), pp. 271–76. Key also puts the Texas pattern into the general Southern political context.

[7] Letter published in the *Hidalgo County Independent,* Edinburg, Texas, March 8, 1929, cited in Weeks, "League," pp. 275–76, cited in Guzmán, "Political Socialization," p. 160.

preceded by a number of changes in the structure of the Mexican American population.

THE POLITICIZATION OF
MEXICAN AMERICANS

The politicization of Mexican American communities in the Southwest dates only from the years following World War II. For the most part politicization was prefaced by deep social changes among the Mexican American population, discussed elsewhere in this book. In sum, they brought Mexicans into new and partly unforeseen contact with American society, particularly in urban areas. The word "urbanization" hardly conveys their impact. A demand for labor brought hundreds of thousands of Mexicans into cities from rural areas, and at the same time many hundreds of thousands of young Mexican American men found themselves in uniform—and racially invisible to Anglos from other areas of the United States and to other peoples in foreign lands. At the same time, however, their families began to find that the urban areas of the Southwest, like rural ones, were highly discriminatory (this was the time of the "zoot suit riots" in Los Angeles and San Diego, California [8]). (In the rural areas, however, the social fabric that supported and justified discrimination was hardly changed.)

In the cities the urban migrants could find only poor housing, the lowest unskilled employment, and restricted access to schools and other public facilities. As before, few Mexican Americans took part in political activity, although the tradition of political accommodation now seemed outmoded. So did the political organizations built to formalize this relationship to the larger community. A middle class had begun to increase rather rapidly as a result of wartime prosperity, and it was increasingly dissatisfied. Against this background a group of articulate former servicemen (helped substantially by the educational and training benefits of the G.I. Bill of Rights) began to press for changes in the community. In Los Angeles a more open environment facilitated a new alliance with labor elements, Anglo civil leaders, and religious leaders.

One outcome of this alliance was the California-based Community

[8] The zoot suit riots were a series of racial incidents in Los Angeles during the summer of 1943—later called "race riots"—between U.S. servicemen and Mexican American youth (also called "pachuco riots"). These battles, the humiliation of Mexican Americans, ensuing mass arrests of Mexicans (*not* of the servicemen who were later shown to have provoked them) had a deep impact on the Mexican American community. It resulted immediately in a sharp increase in Anglo discrimination of all kinds against Mexicans and laid the ground for a deep anger and bitterness among the Mexican American community which had been largely impotent to deal with the situation. McWilliams gives an account of the riots in *North from Mexico*.

Service Organization (CSO). In Los Angeles the CSO tried to develop indigenous leaders to organize community activity around local issues, using the techniques of larger-scale grassroots community organization. In this manner the Community Service Organization mobilized large segments of the Mexican American community into activities directed against restricted housing, police brutality, segregated schools, inequitable justice, and discriminatory employment, all problems endemic in the Mexican American areas of southern California as much as in other parts of the Southwest. In this process CSO became an important and meaningful post-World War II political phenomenon in the Mexican American community.

In general CSO pressed for full and equal rights for Mexican Americans. The new emphasis was the extra appeal for active and increased participation by as many elements of the community as possible. Therefore, in contrast to previous organizations, CSO tended to be more egalitarian. Under the influence of an outside catalyst (Saul Alinsky's Industrial Areas Foundation) it became a group that no longer served as the vehicle of a relatively few and successful Mexican Americans. Although the leadership tended to be new middle class, on the whole it made an effort to recruit members of the working class and other lower-class elements, including new arrivals from Mexico. CSO also had some non-Mexican members, although they were comparatively few.

This idea of an alliance of equals from various strata of Mexican American society became important. In contrast to the paternalism of previous organizations such as LULAC, there was little concern with the assimilation of lower-class elements into the mainstream of American life. Nor, for that matter, did CSO show any interest in "Mexican culture." The guiding idea of CSO was to cope with concrete and immediate social, economic, and political problems.

The founders of CSO assumed that American institutions were basically responsive to the needs and demands of the Mexican American population. There were no questions about the legitimacy of these institutions; it was always assumed that proper community organization and action would force Anglo institutions to respond to the needs of Mexican Americans. Accordingly, getting Mexicans to exercise the right to vote became a prime CSO objective. Members organized large-scale nonpartisan community drives to register voters. In Los Angeles these registration drives rather significantly increased the number of Spanish-surname voters. The immediate results were electoral victories by Mexican American candidates, there and in nearby communities. Furthermore, CSO pressure on public housing authorities, on the Fair Employment Practices Commission (FEPC), and against police brutality also yielded results. Housing authorities eased discriminatory practices, Mexican American representation was included in the FEPC, and the police department agreed "to go easy on Mexicans" on the Los Angeles East Side.

At the time members considered CSO tactics radical and militant, and throughout the 1950s the CSO remained a politically powerful organization that emphasized direct, grassroots community action. Numerous CSO chapters were organized throughout the state of California, each duplicating the Alinsky approach to community organization.

In recent years CSO has declined as a potent community organization, in part because of the withdrawal of financial support from the Industrial Areas Foundation, and in part because it lost some of its most energetic members. For example, the single most well-known former member of CSO, César Chávez, split with the urban-centered CSO to organize a union of farm workers. Also contributing to the decline of CSO was the rise of competing organizations of Mexican Americans.

Other organizations in the Southwest reflect the aggressive political style growing after World War II. In Texas, there is the important American G.I. Forum. The G.I. Forum was founded by a south Texas physician, Dr. Hector Garcia; the immediate cause of its formation was the refusal of a funeral home in Three Rivers, Texas, to bury a Mexican American war veteran in 1948. The incident attracted national attention, and the idea of the G.I. Forum spread rapidly not only in Texas but also throughout the Southwest, to several midwestern states, and to Washington, D.C. Although the Forum is concerned with nonpartisan civic action, it has moved increasingly toward more direct and aggressive political activities. In Texas, where its main strength lies, the G.I. Forum launched intensive "Get out the vote" and "Pay your poll tax" drives in the 1950s. Subsequently, it has continued voter registration drives since the repeal of the Texas poll tax. On a number of other issues, the Forum continues to act as a spokesman against the problems that beset the Mexican American community in Texas.

If the CSO and the American G.I. Forum reflect the goals of the immediate postwar years, two political groups founded in the late 1950s show a shift in both the political goals and the resources available in the community. In California the Mexican American Political Association (MAPA), founded in 1958, and in Texas the Political Association of Spanish-speaking Organizations (PASSO) were organized essentially as groups pressuring the political system at the party level. These were not primarily attempts to organize the Mexican American poor to register and vote; they were efforts to use growing middle-class strength to win concessions for Mexican Americans from the Anglo-dominated political parties. Essentially the goal of both associations was simply to get Mexican Americans into political office, either as nominees for elective office in the regular parties or as appointees of elected Anglo officials. Thus the best-publicized effort of either group was the successful deposition of the Anglo political structure in Crystal City, Texas, in the early 1960s. In this venture, PASSO joined with some non-Mexican groups, notably the Teamsters and the Catholic Bishops' Committee for the Spanish Speaking. (Although the victory in Crystal City was short-lived, it was as significant to Texas Mexicans as the more recent victory of a Negro mayor in Mississippi was to the black community.)

Both MAPA and PASSO gain strength by virtue of their statewide connections, which are particularly important in the outlying rural areas where repression has been a norm. Statewide ties give courage and support to local efforts. (At this writing one of the strongest MAPA chapters in California is the chapter in the Coachella valley, a citrus- and date-growing area not far from Palm Springs. The local chairman, a vociferous spokesman for Mexican American laborers, is constantly subject to harassment. He is also constantly in demand outside the immediate area. The intervention of outside elements in a local and rather repressive situation has reduced isolation and repression. As in Crystal City, one of MAPA's victories has been the election of Mexican American officials in the grower-dominated town of Coachella.)

Although both MAPA and PASSO are still largely confined to California and Texas, respectively, there are branches and organizational efforts in other states. The two associations once considered amalgamation into a regional group; but, incredibly, the effort failed because the two groups could not agree on a common name. Texas Mexicans could not afford the then too overt ethnic pride suggested by "Mexican American," and the California group would not accept the euphemism "Spanish-speaking." At these discussions, one disgusted delegate finally proposed "CACA" (a Spanish equivalent of the English "doo-doo") to represent the "Confederated Alliance of *Chicano* Associations." Interestingly, only in such an intensely in-group situation could the name *Chicano* be suggested. At the time this word could not be used for a serious political discussion.

THE *CHICANO* MOVEMENT

Throughout this chapter we have suggested that Mexican American political activity has often been related to social structural factors. Because much of this political activity was possible only after certain structural changes in Mexican American life, there were seldom any real alternatives beyond simple reaction to Anglo pressure. The importance of the *Chicano* movement as an alternative to pressures from the majority society can hardly be overemphasized. It is a distinctively novel development in the Mexican American community. The *Chicano* movement developed in southern California no earlier than 1966, and it is already a sharp new force in the political expression of Mexican Americans throughout the southwest.

The *Chicano* ideology includes a broad definition of political activity. Ironically, such thinking was possible only for a new generation of urbanized and "Anglicized" (that is, assimilated) young Mexican Americans, who were much less burdened by social and class restrictions than their elders were and whose education had exposed them to new ideas.

The exact beginnings of the movement are obscure. There is some evidence that the *Chicano* movement grew out of a group of conferences held at Loyola University in Los Angeles in the summer of 1966. As originally conceived by its Catholic sponsors, the conferences were to create a fairly innocuous youth organization for the middle-class Mexican students attending various colleges throughout California. Very quickly the movement grew beyond the intent or control of its sponsors (Loyola has never been very noted for its interest in Mexican American education) and it drew in yet others, not students and not middle class, who were attracted by the ideology of *chicanismo*. Thus it cannot be understood as a movement limited to the young, to students, or even to urban areas. It must also be understood as including the followers of Reies Tijerina in northern New Mexico and César Chávez' embattled union of striking farm workers in central California. In 1969 Rodolfo (Corky) González was the principal leader and inspiration of the *Chicano* movement in Denver although his interests were mainly in urban civic action. Moreover, "Corky" has organized regional youth conferences and his influence spreads far beyond the local area. No one leader has yet emerged in southern California or in Texas.

As this wide range of activity shows, the *Chicano* movement is extremely heterogenous, and its elements have different aims and purposes. In this way the movement cuts across social class, regional, and generational lines. Its aims range from traditional forms of social protest to increasingly more radical goals that appear as a sign of an emerging nationalism. It is a social movement, in that it can be described as "pluralistic behavior functioning as an organized mass effort directed toward a change of established folkways or institutions." [9] The dynamic force of the movement is its ideology—*chicanismo*.

9 As defined by Abel, in *Why Hitler Came to Power*, as cited in Martin Oppenheimer, *The Urban Guerilla* (Chicago: Quadrangle Books, 1969), p. 19.

The new ideology is advanced as a challenge to the dominant Anglo beliefs concerning Mexicans as well as to the beliefs of Mexican Americans themselves. Although we have emphasized that students are by no means the only element of the *Chicano* movement, we will reconstruct *chicanismo* primarily as it has been developed among students. Actually, this is only one of several ideological strands but it is the most consistently developed, thus the best illustration of the change from protest to nationalism and a synthesis of the ideology of *chicanismo*.

The first student form of the *Chicano* movement coincided with the development of new student organizations in California universities and colleges in 1966 and 1967. Some of these groups were the United Mexican American Students (UMAS), the Mexican American Student Association (MASA), Mexican American Student Confederation (MASC), and Movimiento Estudiantil Chicano de Aztlán (MECHA). More recently the Mexican American Youth Organization (MAYO) has appeared, with particular strength in Texas. (MAYO is also the name adopted by the new organizations of *Chicanos* in California prisons.) These student groups were at first concerned with a rather narrow range of problems in the field of education, particularly those concerned with increasing the number of Mexican American students in college. To the extent that these student groups were active in the Mexican American community, they were involved with various forms of protest against specific and long-standing grievances, such as police brutality and inferior educational facilities, although other forms of community activity also involved political campaigns.

Chicano student groups thus have never repudiated ordinary forms of political activity, although for them such forms as voting constitute only one political alternative. Actually, given the wide range of problems facing the Mexican American community, *Chicanos* view conventional forms of political activity as perhaps the least effective. Instead, they favor forms of confrontation as the most effective means to gain access for the traditionally excluded *Chicano,* even though it has, on occasion, led to violence. In general, this conception of politics contrasts sharply with the ideas of more conservative Mexican American leaders, most of whom adhere to very limited and "safe" politics with an emphasis on voting and "working within the system" to gain political leverage. This is not to say that *Chicanos* reject working for social change within the system; as a matter of fact, much recent activity has focussed on bringing about change in the universities and colleges as well as in the public school systems. Nevertheless, whereas the moderates seek to bring major change in American society through nonviolent means, the more militant speak of the need for "revolutionary activity," though they often leave the details and direction of this revolution unspecified. While they admire the life style and aspirations of revolutionary leaders like Ché Guevara, they have thus far made no systematic theoretical connection between the *Chicano* movement and the general literature on revolution. The theoretical underpinnings of the *Chicano* movement thus often lack a strong direction.

And yet, the advent of the *Chicano* movement does represent a revolutionary phenomenon among Mexican Americans. As we shall see, most of the change from traditional forms lies in (or is reflected in) the ideology of *chicanismo*. Basically eclectic, *chicanismo* draws inspiration from outside the United States and outside the Mexican American experience. The Cuban Revolution, for example, exerts some influence, as do the career and ideals of Ché Guevera. For instance, the Brown Berets (a *Chicano* youth group) affect the life style of this revolutionary. Black Power also offers something of a model. Most recently, *Chicanos* have resurrected the Mexican revolutionary tradition.

Basically, however, *chicanismo* focuses on the life experience of the Mexican in the United States. It challenges the belief system of the majority society at the same time that it attempts to reconstruct a new image for Mexican Americans themselves. *Chicanos* assume that along with American Indians and black Americans, Mexicans live in the United States as a conquered people. This idea allows *chicanismo* to explain the evolution of the *Chicano* as essentially conflictful. In each conflictual relationship with Anglos, the Mexicans lost out and were thus forced to live in the poverty and degradation attendant upon those with the status of a conquered people. This is no better illustrated than by the Mexicans' loss of communal and private property. As a result, they had no choice but to work the land for a *patrón* (usually an Anglo, but sometimes a Mexican, who exploited his own people). When the Mexican was thrown off the land, he was forced to become an unattached wage-earner, often a migrant farm worker; or he might migrate to a city, where the exploitation continued. In any event, *chicanismo* emphasizes that the Mexican was transformed into a rootless economic commodity, forced either to depend on migrant farm work or to sell his labor in the urban centers, where his fate depended upon the vicissitudes of the economy. Ironically, indispensable as Mexican labor was for the economic development of the Southwest, the Mexican got little recognition for his contribution and even less benefit from it.

Chicanos therefore see the economic expansion of the Southwest as essentially a dehumanizing process. They also point out that during periods of economic depression in the United States, when the Mexican became "superfluous" and "expensive," Anglo society had no qualms about attempting to eliminate Mexicans from the United States, as in the repatriations of the 1930s (see Chapter Three). The repatriations are viewed as a conscious attempt to eliminate the *Chicano* from American society.

The thrust of *chicanismo* is not only economic, but also cultural. In many ways, the exploitation and suppression of his culture is what most angers the *Chicano,* who views the attempt to deracinate Mexican culture in the Southwest as the reason why Mexican Americans are disoriented about their culture and often attempt to deny it. The *Chicano* points out that the Anglo himself often views Mexicans with a great degree of ambivalence. Anglos oftentimes take over aspects of "Spanish" (which is really Mexican) culture and at the same time deny it to the Mexican himself. In this fashion Mexicans were denied the development of a more autonomous cultural life, especially as it touches upon Spanish language use, the arts, and so on. (This was done in spite of the agreements made in the signing of the Treaty of Guadalupe Hidalgo. Early drafts of the treaty contained Mexican government efforts to make formal recognition of language rights for Mexicans who chose to remain in the United States after the Mexican War. These provisions were not approved by the U.S. Senate.)

Worse yet, the ideology goes on, the cultural suppression continues to the present day, reinforced by Anglo institutions, particularly the schools. The extreme position (although by no means infrequent) is represented by the fact that Mexican American students in the public schools are corporally punished for using Spanish, their native language. Under these circumstances, it is understandable that the Mexican American student remains ignorant and often ashamed of his past. When the Mexican is mentioned in textbooks, it is in a romanticized and stereotypically Anglicized version of "Spanish culture" that may be congenial to Anglos but is remote and irrelevant to the Mexican American. The *Chicano* considers this type of whitewashed "Spanish" culture particularly galling because he feels that while Anglos may selectively choose certain motifs from Mexican culture, the person behind the culture, the Mexican himself, is given neither recognition nor respect.

Chicanismo also focuses on race, and in some ways this emphasis constitutes one of the most controversial aspects of *chicanismo.* It is argued that Anglo racism denies the Mexican his ethnicity by making him ashamed of his "Mexican-ness." Mexican ancestry, instead of being a source of pride, becomes a symbol of shame and inferiority. As a consequence, Mexicans spend their lives apologizing or denying their ancestry, to the point that many dislike and resent being called "Mexican," preferring "Spanish American," "Latin," "Latin American," and similar euphemisms. For these reasons, the term *"Chicano"* is now insisted upon by activists as a symbol of the new assertiveness.

Advocates of *chicanismo* therefore hope to reconstruct the Mexican Americans' concept of themselves by appeals to pride of a common history, culture and "race." *Chicanismo* attempts to redefine the Mexicans' identity on the basis not of class, generation, or area of residence but on a unique and shared experience in the United States. This means that appeals for political action, economic progress, and reorientation of cultural identity are cast in terms of the common history, culture, and ethnic background of *la raza*.

Chicano ideologues insist that social advance based on material achievement is, in the final analysis, less important than social advance based on *la raza;* they reject what they call the myth of American individualism. The *Chicano* movement feels that it cannot afford the luxury of individualism; if Mexicans are to confront the problems of their group realistically they must begin to act along collective lines. Hence, the stirrings of a new spirit of what *chicanismo* terms "cultural nationalism" among the Mexican Americans of the Southwest.

Chicanismo has led not only to increased participation in community activities, but also to a heightened and often intense interest in cultural life. *Chicano* poets, playwrights, journalists, and writers of all varieties have suddenly appeared. There are *Chicano* theater groups in several large cities (often known as the *teatro urbano*) and one nationally known and well-travelled group from Delano, California (*El teatro campesino*), which tells the story not only of the striking California farmworkers but of *Chicanos* in general. Newspapers and magazines also reflect this desire to disseminate the idea of *chicanismo*. Throughout the Southwest numerous *Chicano* "underground" newspapers and magazines publishing literary materials have emerged. There is even a *Chicano* Press Association, a regional association representing *Chicano* publications from Texas to California. Furthermore, because of the strong base in colleges and universities, a serious and generally successful drive to develop "ethnic studies" programs has appeared, especially in California. As part of the drive to spread the idea of *chicanismo* in education, *Chicanos* place an emphasis on Mexican contributions to American society, thus giving *Chicano* college students a new conception of their past and present.

Chicano student groups share an orientation similar to that of black students, and on occasion they cooperate and support each other on similar demands. (There is more mutual support between black and brown students than between their counterparts at the community level.) The alliance between black and brown students, however, has not been close, harmonious, or continuous. *Chicano* student organizations have not yet been significantly involved with Anglo radical student groups, although these groups sometimes claim their support or claim that they are working for the benefit of *Chicanos*.

THE ECHO OF *CHICANISMO*

How much has this student manifestation of the *Chicano* movement affected the larger Mexican community? At this writing the ideological reverberations have been considerable, particularly among the young people of college age and including also those in the secondary schools. We must not forget that the Mexican American population is very young. Some counterparts of *Chicano* college militancy have appeared throughout the Southwest in high schools as, for example, among students in Denver, Los Angeles, San Francisco, and many smaller cities.

The demands have often been modest, in most instances no more than for increased counselling services for Mexican American students and other changes in the methods and content of instruction. In some Texas cities and in Denver, Colorado, the student militants further demanded the end of punishment for using Spanish on the school grounds. In most cases the school boards have acceded to this particular demand. But the reaction of the Anglo community has often been fierce. In Los Angeles a school "walk-out" by Mexican American students in 1968 resulted in the arrest of 13 alleged leaders for criminal conspiracy. In Denver a sharp reaction by the police resulted in the injury of 17 persons and the arrest of 40. In other areas in the Southwest there have been similar, if less publicized, responses to *Chicano* militancy.

Neither the Anglo reaction nor the rapid spread of *chicanismo* should be taken to mean that a full-blown social movement is in progress among Mexican Americans. In many areas, on the contrary, established Mexican American leaders have dissociated themselves from the *Chicanos*. For instance, a school walkout by Mexican students in Kingsville, Texas brought an angry denunciation from a Mexican American Congressman from Texas and other community leaders. At the same time, the *Chicano* movement poses a very difficult dilemma for most older Mexican Americans. They sympathize with the goals of *chicanismo*, yet they fear that the radical means used to pursue these ends will undermine their own hard-earned social and economic gains. The Anglo community expects a denunciation of what it considers to be irresponsible acts of these young people. But for the older leaders to oppose the *Chicano* protest might be a slow form of personal political suicide as well as acting to exacerbate divisiveness in the Mexican American community.

In California, *Chicano* student groups have grown rapidly; they have acquired the power to pass on Mexican American faculty appointments in many high schools and colleges. Typically such faculty members are avidly sought to assist with the new ethnic studies programs and centers. Ultimately, though, *Chicano* students are faced by responsibility to the community. These students are aware that the popularity of *chicanismo* among Mexican American students means a major opportunity for the development of an entire new generation of young professionals to carry these ideas back to the Mexican American community.

Beyond the universities there have been other sources of support, some of them quite substantial. Grants and direct organizing assistance have come from American Protestant denominations, notably the National Council of Churches. In 1968 a substantial ($630,000) grant from the Ford Foundation to the Southwest Council of La Raza (headquarters in Phoenix) helped the organization of a number of militant *Chicano* groups. The Southwest Council of La Raza considers itself permanent and accepts money for *"barrio* development" from not only the Ford Foundation but churches, labor groups, and other interested organizations. Both the announced ideals of the council and its membership assure commitment to the ideals of *chicanismo.*

The *Chicano* movement began as a protest. Only later did its dynamics carry it toward an increasing cultural nationalism. The first steps toward social change did not go beyond demands for equality of opportunity for Mexican Americans, which are still being made (by the less militant in the movement). Until recently no Mexican American had tried to define the problems of the community in any terms except those of assimilation. It is precisely these ideas of assimilation and social "adjustment" that the *Chicano* militant rejects. As a new alternative, *chicanismo* represents a conception of an autonomous and self-determining social life for Mexican Americans.

It is interesting that it was not until the 1960s that the *Chicano* leaders emerged to question some of the oldest and most fundamental assumptions of Mexicans in American society. This protest probably would not have been possible in a period of general social calm and stability. That the *Chicano* protest emerged when it did is perhaps due in large part to the emergence of other social groups that also began to question basic notions about American society. But if these other groups feel a sense of alienation in American society, the *Chicano's* alienation is doubly acute. It is not only from American society that he feels alienated; he also feels left out of the mainstream of Mexican history and, simultaneously, he feels a sense of guilt for having "deserted" the homeland. It is this sense of being in two cultures yet belonging to neither (*ni aqui ni allá*) that is the source of his most profound alienation and now, anger. It is against this background that the *Chicano* is attempting with a deep sense of urgency to reconstruct his history, his culture, his sense of identity.

In practical terms the result is increasing radicalization, with which comes a new set of problems. Cultural nationalism has emerged, bringing with it questions that must be answered if the *Chicano* movement is to become a potent force for all Mexican Americans in their diverse circumstances throughout the Southwest and other parts of the United States.

Epilogue

In his recent book on American income and labor force distribution, Herman Miller has this to say about Mexican Americans:

> Spanish Americans have generally had a very good press.... Their plight has been well publicized and considerable sympathy—well deserved —has been engendered. In the process, unfortunately, the impression has been created that their plight is worse than that of Negroes and other minority groups on the West Coast.... They are ... better off than most non-whites.[1]

A recent issue of *Time* magazine devoted to poverty in the United States, mentioned Mexican Americans only in passing in an article covering many pages.[2] Almost no Mexicans were invited to the 1965 White House Conference on Civil Rights.

Miller's statement is misleading on two counts. Mexican Americans are not "better off than most non-whites," and it is not true that Mexicans have had a "good press." They have had almost no press whatsoever. Even the few remarks that occasionally slip into national publications were not enough to show Miller that only a few Mexicans are—or want to be—called "Spanish Americans." In spite of the fact that Mexican Americans by all measures of income, occupational distribution, and housing are America's second largest disadvantaged minority (far outnumbering the more widely known Indians and Puerto Ricans) a national news magazine has yet no idea that Mexicans are a substantial part of the nation's poor. (The map accompanying the *Time* article designated south Texas and New Mexico as areas of concentrated poverty but without mentioning the inhabitants.) The national civil rights conference simply ignored them in spite of the persistence of a massive civil rights problem.[3]

1 Herman P. Miller, *Rich Man, Poor Man* (New York: Thomas Y. Crowell Company, New American Library, Signet Book edition, 1964), p. 128.
2 *Time*, Vol. 91, No. 20 (May 17, 1968), 24–35.
3 In the fall of 1968, a Los Angeles County Grand Jury indicted 13 Mexican Americans on criminal conspiracy charges. One of the strategies of the defense attorneys

Nor has the "good press" been eloquent enough to get Mexicans included in all the standard textbooks about American ethnic groups that are used on either the high school or the college level. Truly the Mexican Americans are a "second minority"—a footnote to discussions of failures in the American dream.

It may be this characteristic of being "second" in nearly every way that accounts for the curious invisibility of the Mexican Americans. In some way they are similar to nearly every other ethnic group in the nation. They are also distinctive in many ways, but overshadowed in a nation preoccupied in at least the past decade with the black minority. Perhaps their plight can best be summed up as a series of contradictions.

Mexicans are very nearly the oldest and yet the newest minority. Mexican immigrants settled in the upper Rio Grande valley of New Mexico a full generation before the Plymouth colony. Descendants of those colonies never left New Mexico. On the other hand, no other group entered the United States in as large numbers from 1930 to 1960 and is still immigrating (both legally and illegally) at such a considerable rate.

No other minority has been involved in a direct military assault upon the United States government. It is true that Negro riots are now almost commonplace but even the Black Panthers to this date have rarely taken the initiative in aggression. By contrast, in June of 1967 a band of more than 50 armed Mexican Americans assaulted the Rio Arriba County Courthouse in Tierra Amarilla, New Mexico. Yet the masses of Mexican Americans in the large cities of the Southwest are politically inert. The very model of Mexican leadership has been the "quiet fighter," who does not create any public difficulties. Until the arrival of César Chávez in 1965 and the dramatic agricultural strikes in the San Joaquin valley in California and in the Rio Grande valley in Texas, the "Mexican way" was quiet and private negotiation, no more. Demonstrations have been few. At this writing Mexican American sympathy with the Negro civil rights movement is scattered and scarcely respectable.

Mexicans have no very clear consensus on whether they are a racial group, a cultural group, or even if they are white or nonwhite. Yet the idea of *la raza* permeates the Mexican American population. *"La raza"* does not refer to "race" at all, but to a vague sense of ethnic identity,

---

was a motion to quash the indictment on the grounds that the Grand Jury showed a gross underrepresentation of Spanish-surname persons over the previous 10 years. The hearing on the motion entailed questioning some 30 Superior Court judges who nominate jurors. Most of these judges testified that most of them had never asked Mexican Americans (or thought of asking them) because they were unacquainted with them. It became evident in the course of their testimony that most of them never seriously considered Mexican Americans as a problem.

a compelling feeling of belonging—but to *what* is left relatively uncon-
ceptualized. For their part, Anglos long thought of Mexicans as a racial
group, but the Mexicans themselves have always shown much ambivalence
in their attitudes toward the predominantly *mestizo* strain. Spanish blood
was always carefully distinguished from the Indian stock. The confusion
is not confined to the Mexicans. Although there were never miscegena-
tion statutes or other legal discrimination, as there were against Filipinos
and Negroes, for example, segregation has been widespread and pervasive, and discrimination equally so. Only very slowly has the consciousness of discrimination become legitimated among Mexican American
spokesmen: only very slowly have they been willing to define the Mexican Americans as a minority and to risk the pejorative implications of
such a definition.

The minority includes peons—but also aristocrats. Some Mexican
Americans, for example the Canary Islanders of San Antonio, are aristocrats who consider themselves such, and are accepted as such by white
Americans. But they and even the small (but growing) middle class are
overshadowed by the desperately poor, an underclass exemplified by thousands of stricken families in the large cities of the Southwest and by the
migrant farm laborers, who still perform agricultural tasks throughout
the Southwest.

Mexicans include both the assimilated and the unassimilated. Full
acceptance into American life is available for many. In Los Angeles the
middle-class, third generation young people intermarry with native Anglos
to a large degree. On the other hand there are still large Mexican enclaves,
particularly in certain counties in Colorado, New Mexico, and Texas,
where ethnic exclusiveness is almost complete—even among middle-class
individuals who have lived for many generations in the United States.

It is precisely these contradictions that create special dilemmas for
Mexican immigrants and their children, who can usually see both alternatives at once. In terms of models, the Mexican American can hope for
assimilation. He can also hope to be accepted into the upper class of a
semi-caste. He can remain very nearly completely Mexican, returning frequently to Mexico. He can become a tough young militant on the black
power model. He can even withdraw completely from any form of collective action as, in fact, have most middle-class Mexican Americans; be a
Colonist or a Frontiersman.

It is this diversity that makes any characterization of Mexican Americans so extremely difficult. Unfortunately, most Americans can think
about groups like America's Mexicans in only two ways. One is in terms
of the classic and seemingly inevitable merger of the immigrant into the

mainstream of the American life. The other is the familiar current situation of the black American. But neither of these ways of thinking describes the Mexican American in the United States, who stands somewhere between.

Selected Bibliography

Clark, Margaret, *Health in the Mexican-American Culture: A Community Study.* Berkeley, Calif.: University of California Press, 1959.
A study of a poor Mexican American *barrio* in San Jose, focussing on the "culture of health," but covering many other facets of community life.

Colorado Commission on Spanish Surnamed Citizens, *The Status of Spanish Surnamed Citizens in Colorado: Report to the Colorado General Assembly.* Greeley, Colo: 1967.
A comprehensive summary of knowledge on Spanish Americans in Colorado, including abstracts of current research, often critical.

Galarza, Ernesto, *Merchants of Labor: The Mexican Bracero Story.* San Jose, Calif.: Rosicrucian Press, 1965.
History of the *bracero* program and related issues, by one of the most important labor organizers working in agriculture.

González, Nancie L., *The Spanish Americans of New Mexico: A Distinctive Heritage.* Advance Report 9, Mexican-American Study Project. Los Angeles: University of California, 1967.
Thorough overview of the "peculiar" New Mexican situation, with a historical approach, though done by an anthropologist. Includes a comprehensive bibliography.

Grebler, Leo, Joan W. Moore, and Ralph C. Guzmán, et al., *The Mexican American People: The Nation's Second Largest Minority.* New York: The Free Press-Macmillan, 1970.
Broad analysis of the Mexican Americans in the Southwest, focussing on the urban situation. Includes thorough analysis of census data and data from community surveys. Much of the material in this volume, *Mexican Americans,* is drawn from this larger study.

Inter-Agency Committee on Mexican American Affairs. *The Mexican Americans: A New Focus on Opportunity.* Testimony Presented at the Cabinet Committee Hearings on Mexican American Affairs, El Paso, Texas, October 26–28, 1967. Washington, D.C.: n. d.
Mexican Americans speak for themselves. Spokesmen, almost all Mexican American, present their analyses of current problems and remedies, geared toward action.

McWilliams, Carey. *North from Mexico: The Spanish-speaking People of the United States.* New York: J. B. Lippincott Co., 1949.

Recently reissued, this was one of the earliest attempts to "present" the Mexican Americans broadly. Includes some primary-source material relating to Los Angeles.

Pitt, Leonard. *The Decline of the Californios: A Social History of the Spanish-Speaking Californians, 1846–1890.* Los Angeles: University of California Press, 1966.
The title is self-explanatory.

Robinson, Cecil. *With the Ears of Strangers: The Mexican in American Literature.* Tucson, Ariz.: University of Arizona Press, 1963.
Presents a number of summaries of portrayals of Mexicans and Mexican Americans, ranging from "impressions" of the early American explorers through portrayals in contemporary fiction.

Rubel, Arthur J. *Across the Tracks: Mexican-Americans in a Texas City.* Austin, Tex.: University of Texas Press, 1966.
Good community study of a South Texas border town. Like Clark's, the focus is on health but the coverage is broad.

Saunders, Lyle. *Cultural Differences and Medical Care: The Case of the Spanish-Speaking People of the Southwest.* New York: Russell Sage Foundation, 1954.
Like Clark's and Rubel's books, focussed on health but with a broad scope: the author's sociological approach differs from the other two books.

Tuck, Ruth D. *Not with the Fist: Mexican-Americans in a Southwest City.* New York: Harcourt, Brace and Co., 1956.
Good study of Mexican Americans in San Bernardino, California, a large city, presenting a deep study of Mexican Americans in the post World War II period.

Woods, Sister Frances Jerome. *Mexican Ethnic Leadership in San Antonio, Texas.* Washington, D.C.: The Catholic University of America Press, 1949.
Historical analysis of the position of Mexican Americans in San Antonio, with a focus on the position of the Mexican American political leadership in the city's social structure.

In addition to the above, there are a number of periodicals stemming from the *Chicano* movement. *El Malcriado* is published monthly by the United Farm Workers Organizing Committee, César Chávez' union (P.O. Box 130, Delano, California, 93215). *El Grito* is a literary-scholarly quarterly published at the University of California, Berkeley. *Con Safos* is a literary-political journal (P.O. Box 31085, Los Angeles, 90031). The Chicano Press Association is a news service serving a number of newspapers, such as *La Raza* in Los Angeles.

Index

167